A LIFE OF
LIES AND
SPIES

A LIFE OF LIES AND SPIES

Tales of a CIA Covert Ops Polygraph Interrogator

Alan B. Trabue

Thomas Dunne Books   St. Martin's Press   New York

THOMAS DUNNE BOOKS.
An imprint of St. Martin's Press.

www.thomasdunnebooks.com
www.stmartins.com

Designed by Meryl Sussman Levavi

The Library of Congress Cataloging-in-Publication Data is available upon request.

ISBN 978-1-250-06504-9 (hardcover)
ISBN 978-1-4668-7155-7 (e-book)

St. Martin's Press books may be purchased for educational, business, or promotional use. For information on bulk purchases, please contact the Macmillan Corporate and Premium Sales Department at 1-800-221-7945, extension 5442, or write to specialmarkets@macmillan.com.

First Edition: June 2015

10 9 8 7 6 5 4 3 2 1

A significant portion of my life has been spent gallivanting around the world for the CIA. Unfortunately, a lifetime of travel caused me to miss many of life's wonderful moments with my wife and daughter—moments that will be lost forever. I was away on almost every kind of holiday, birthday, and anniversary celebrated by my family. Lengthy absences from home forced me to burden my wife, Sharon, with many of life's miseries that we should have tackled together. Without her love and support, my nomadic lifestyle would not have been possible. My career path would have been quite different, and I would have had far fewer adventures. I am a romantic who was lucky enough to find the love of his life early in life. Sharon is incredibly supportive and understanding. More importantly, she gives meaning to Marilyn Monroe's words, "A career is wonderful, but you can't curl up with it on a cold night." She is my island of tranquility in the storm of life, and I will be eternally grateful for her partnership in the exceptionally bizarre way I chose to make a living. This book is dedicated to my wife, Sharon.

Contents

Acknowledgments

I would like to acknowledge several people for their help during the writing of *A Life of Lies and Spies*. What began as a solitary experience eventually turned into a team effort. I would like to thank my literary agent, Greg Aunapu, of the Salkind Literary Agency. His enthusiastic review and generous feedback were greatly appreciated, and I will forever remember when he said, "It's a real honor to have one's career monumentalized as a book."

Editor Rob Kirkpatrick, assistant Jennifer Letwack, and copy editor David Stanford Burr of Thomas Dunne Books deserve special thanks for their expertise in polishing my manuscript.

Obligated by a CIA secrecy agreement, I am grateful for the prompt and judicious review of my manuscript by the CIA Publications Review Board.

Friends and family merit special mention. My training trip partner and friend of forty years deserves special acknowledgment for being the role model that set me on the right path in our profession. To all my friends and colleagues, I sincerely welcomed your kind words and support during the writing of my memoir. Finally, I cannot find the words to adequately express my appreciation for the love and support of my wife, Sharon, and our daughter, Lisa.

A LIFE OF LIES AND SPIES

Chapter One

Ready, Aim . . .

Oh what a tangled web we weave,
When first we practice to deceive!
—SIR WALTER SCOTT

T he day was supposed to be a routine travel day between CIA offices, a simple one-hour flight from the international airport in a Southeast Asian capital city to another city up-country. It was 1976, and as a CIA covert ops polygraph examiner, I had made hundreds of similar trips in the past without incident. By midmorning, it had gone terribly wrong.

The day started off as planned. After an hour-long taxi ride to the airport, I checked in at the airline counter and made my way to the departure lounge carrying my briefcase. I didn't normally carry my briefcase, because it really wasn't a briefcase. It was a polygraph instrument built into a briefcase. A casual observer would never know what was inside. Up to that point, my day had gone as expected. I busied myself people-watching in the departure lounge while waiting for the boarding announcement. However, as I watched with disbelieving eyes, soldiers entered the lounge carrying two things that made my heart sink: submachine guns and a table. Terrifying visions of being handcuffed and carried off to jail by armed soldiers filled my mind. I knew my polygraph instrument was very incriminating evidence of espionage, and I didn't have any credentials that would protect me.

The table was set up near the exit door and an announcement followed that passengers would have to submit to a bag search before boarding the airplane. I couldn't believe my bad luck. Should I try to escape by leaving the departure lounge or would that raise their suspicions? That course of action seemed uncomfortably similar to a car approaching a roadblock and turning around to avoid the police. That never has a good outcome. Should I try to bluster my way through as a pompous, overbearing, ugly American? Should I refuse to open my briefcase? All options seemed to lead to the same disastrous conclusion. I decided to cooperate as best I could. Realizing the uproar that would surely ensue when I opened the briefcase, I thought it best to be the last one in line. I wanted as small an audience as possible. So, while other passengers rushed to form some semblance of a line, I hung back and waited. My mind raced, but I was unable to figure out how to escape the terrible predicament. I had no choice but to comply with the security check. One by one, the passengers were screened and allowed to walk out onto the tarmac to climb the steps to the airplane. When I was the last passenger in the departure lounge, I could wait no longer. Walking up to the flimsy table, I put the heavy briefcase down. It caught the immediate attention of a soldier. He motioned for me to open the case. I unsnapped the latches holding the lid closed and spread the briefcase wide open. Looking down, he gasped for air, stepped back, and tightened his grip on the submachine gun. Pointing it straight at my chest, he screamed for help. Terrified, he gripped his weapon so tightly his knuckles turned white. Beads of sweat dotted his forehead and fear widened his eyes. He was one finger twitch away from cutting me in half.

A mere twenty-four hours before, I had taken every step to ensure that this very event would not take place. This was not supposed to be happening. The main office had an urgent need to have an agent polygraphed at one of its smaller offices up-country. Since there was no polygraph instrument stored at the office and insufficient time to send one through official channels, I knew I would have to take an instrument with me on the flight. In the 1970s, a rash of airplane hijackings resulted in passenger and baggage security checks at many international airports. At first, they concentrated on international flights. Few airports were performing security checks on domestic flights. Since my flight was going to be a short domestic flight, I knew that

I could either hand-carry the polygraph instrument on the airplane or pack it in a larger suitcase and send it through as checked baggage. Everything depended on whether the airport had instituted security checks for domestic flights.

"What's the security check situation at the airport?" I asked the case officer.

"There is no security check on domestic flights, only on international flights," he responded with what seemed like a great deal of confidence.

Realizing that I would be in a significant amount of trouble if the polygraph instrument was opened and inspected by security personnel, I wanted to have as much confidence in his answer as he did. After all, an analog polygraph instrument with all its knobs and dials might look like a bomb to an unsophisticated security guard. On the other hand, a more sophisticated security guard might recognize it as a polygraph instrument and wonder what I was doing with spy equipment.

"Hey, I don't feel very comfortable hand-carrying the instrument on an airplane. It's not that I'm unwilling, but this could be dangerous. Can you imagine the commotion it would cause if the briefcase was opened?"

He told me not to worry, but his feeble attempt to reassure me was not very convincing.

Noticing that I still seemed worried, he said, "Alan, relax. I'll check with 'our man' at the airport. He'll have the skinny on the most up-to-date policies and procedures."

He made the call (at least, he said he made the call) and reported to me later in the day that "our man" at the airport confirmed that security checks were only performed on international flights. I thanked him for the extra effort he took to ease my concerns. With this new information, I decided it would be easiest for me to just hand-carry the polygraph instrument on the flight.

I watched another soldier approach to assist the screaming soldier who seemed ready to shoot me. The two spoke excitedly. The second soldier started poking around the contents of my opened polygraph instrument. Chains, tubing, cuffs, finger plates, and ink bottles—it was a playground for a curious mind. He flipped switches and turned knobs. What an incredibly stupid thing to do if the instrument had actually been a bomb.

In the best nonchalant manner I could muster under the circumstances, I smiled and said, "It's for a doctor. It's medical equipment."

My explanation might have fooled them if they understood English. The second soldier called for help. Both pointed their guns at my chest while they waited for help to arrive. Only a table-width away from me, one of those weapons could have cut me in two in an instant. A third soldier approached. Now, two of them poked around the strange-looking contents they had discovered. The first soldier nervously kept his gun aimed straight at me. He was the one that worried me the most.

Still barely able to take my eyes off the menacing submachine guns, in a calm, yet emphatic tone I said once again, "It's for a doctor. It's medical equipment."

It was obvious from their puzzled looks and frightened demeanor, they didn't understand me. Talking back and forth at length, their discussion seemed to turn into an argument. It appeared there was disagreement among the three soldiers about what to do. It must have been their first experience dealing with a mad, American bomber. Their discussion grew loud, high pitched, and agitated. They gestured wildly with their arms and weapons. I didn't understand a word they said, but their demeanor was very threatening. I hoped their argument was not over whether to shoot me or arrest me.

A submachine gun was pointed at me at all times. Eventually, one of them motioned for me to hand over the passport in my hand. After what seemed like an eternity, the guns were pointed away from me, my passport was returned, and they finally motioned for me to board the plane. I packed up the equipment in record time and walked across the tarmac to the waiting airplane. My encounter with the soldiers had delayed its departure. Flight personnel standing at the airplane's door stared at me as I walked up the steps. Passengers glared at me through the windows. As I boarded the airplane and walked down the aisle to my seat, all eyes were on me. I was the center of attention and the object of much whispered speculation. Beads of sweat on my forehead were not caused by the heat. The airplane door was still open. The soldiers could change their minds, rush the airplane, and drag me out. It seemed to take the flight crew forever to prepare for takeoff. They walked slowly down the aisle checking passengers' seatbelts. I kept looking out the window for soldiers running onto the tarmac. Mercifully, the door was finally closed and locked, and the plane began pulling away from the terminal.

After takeoff, most of the passengers stopped staring at me. As the plane continued to climb, I reflected on the terrifying incident. I couldn't get it out of my mind. I thought of my wife and daughter thousands of miles away. I was alone and on my own. A tall, light-skinned foreigner, I stood out like a sore thumb. And I was carrying around a briefcase with contents that looked like a bomb. I wondered how I got myself into this mess. What was it about covert ops? Was it the adrenaline rush from interrogating liars or the challenge of operating clandestinely in hostile environments? With arrest and imprisonment always just around the corner, why would I choose to be a globe-trotting polygraph interrogator for the CIA?

Chapter Two

Welcome to My World of Lies and Spies

Sin has many tools, but a lie is the handle
which fits them all.

— OLIVER WENDELL HOLMES

When I was in charge of the CIA Polygraph School in the 1980s, I used to tell a polygraph joke to new students:

Polygraph training was tough back in the old days. It was very, very tough! It wasn't like it is now. In the old days, they made us put twelve marbles in our mouths when we started training. That was done to make sure we appreciated how hard the job was. When we conducted interviews and interrogations with marbles in our mouths, it was tough. It was incredibly tough! But, when we graduated, we got to take a marble out. When we became a journeyman examiner, we got to take a marble out. When we became a team leader, we got to take a marble out. When we became a branch chief, we got to take a marble out. So, now you know why they say, "Anyone who has been in polygraph for over twenty years must have lost all his marbles!"

The joke usually got a good laugh, although I'm not above admitting that some probably gave it a courtesy chuckle out of respect for the experienced instructor telling the joke.

I watched that twenty-year mark come and go an awfully long time ago. Thirty-eight of my forty years with the CIA were spent in the polygraph program. When I started with the CIA in 1971, I had no prior training or experience in interviewing, interrogation, and polygraph. At that time, I had no grand plan to spend thirty-eight years of my life specializing in the polygraph profession.

I'm an Agency Brat. Unlike the negative connotation that sometimes goes with the moniker, Army Brat, an Agency Brat is typically proud to be so recognized. I don't think carrying on a family tradition meant quite as much to me when I first started with the CIA. I wasn't bursting with pride and didn't feel any sense of honor by walking in my father's footsteps. However, now that I have occasion to reflect back on forty years, I realize I could not be more proud. My father's career with the CIA lasted twenty-three years. They were twenty-three good years, for the most part. A support officer, he had family-accompanied tours of duty in South America, the Far East, and on Saipan, a tiny tropical island in the Pacific Ocean. I realized that filling his shoes would be no small task when I encountered people in countries all over the world who asked, "Are you related to Doug Trabue?" When they learned I was his son, they always smiled broadly and regaled me with tales of friendship and great admiration for his professionalism. Although I did not set out to follow in my father's footsteps, I have become immeasurably proud that I took the journey.

During my time in the polygraph program, I was involved in just about everything the profession had to offer. My experience ran the gamut of going through polygraph training to managing polygraph training, from conducting thousands of polygraph tests to supervising others who conducted tests, and from working in all the polygraph programs to managing all the polygraph programs.

My career conducting tests at home and abroad on applicants, contractors, employees, and foreign agents generated many bizarre experiences. I encountered examinees so fearful, they fainted during their tests and slid out of their chairs. All kinds of personalities generated different responses under the stress of a polygraph exam. There were the fearful ones, the angry ones, and the dangerous ones. There were examinees so stressed, they spewed vomit across the examination room. Terrified examinees fled the examination room, while others were so angry they refused to leave. Angry subjects waited in the parking lot after their polygraph interviews to confront their examiners as they exited the building. Some subjects provided admissions so egregious that they were considered to be a threat to national security and the FBI was called in before they were released. Some subjects admitted to physically abusing and sexually molesting others. When the admissions involved impending harm to others, law enforcement officers were sometimes waiting for the examinees when they returned home. Some have actually stalked their examiners. There were examinees who urinated onto the carpet when their examiner stepped out of the room for a few minutes. One examinee urinated into a tissue box on the examiner's bookcase.

Confessions I extracted from polygraph subjects were numerous, frequent, and varied and sometimes consisted of horrific, gut-wrenching tales that sickened the hardiest of polygraph examiners. Murder, rape, child molestation, incest, wife beating, bestiality, burglary, robbery, theft, assault, fraud, illegal drug use, prostitution, concealing contacts with foreign intelligence services, concealing foreign national contacts, unauthorized revelation of classified information, concealing significant personal history and medical information—whatever illegal activity people can do has been discussed during CIA polygraph tests. Unfortunately, there are mean-spirited people in this world who set out in life to use and abuse others. They will lie, cheat, steal, and break any law to get what they want.

Polygraph is a strange and unique profession—a most demanding and bizarre way to make a living. Many people can't handle the stress it can bring. As one would expect from such a profession, there are stories to be told. There must be a million stories about the applicant program, the reinvestigation program, and the industrial program; but the program with no equal is the covert operations program. The covert operations polygraph program supports the CIA's attempts to validate recruited foreign national agents. In the eyes of their countrymen, most of the agents I polygraphed and interrogated were traitors who sold out their governments for money. Sometimes, well-meaning, idealistic patriots commit espionage, but more often it is the scum of the earth who betray their country. However, an agent's motivation to work secretly for the CIA is seldom as important as the veracity and value of the information he provides. From my perspective, it matters not whether an agent is a patriot or a money-seeking opportunist, for it is the distinctive nature of covert ops polygraph that makes a fine breeding ground for fascinating stories. Foreign countries with unfamiliar settings, languages, and customs; threats of arrest necessitating enhanced security and clandestine meetings; and case outcomes that can impact U.S. and foreign policy—all contribute to the foreign intrigue that frames a great tale.

Conducting covert cases overseas was a stepping-stone that eventually led to my selection as manager of the CIA's worldwide covert operations polygraph program. The assignment turned out to be the opportunity of a lifetime. It offered, and delivered, adventure and excitement. Unfortunately, there are aspects to any adventure that are less than glorious. I remember times when I was absolutely miserable and afraid, wishing to be anywhere else and to be doing anything else at the time. An adventure is something to boast of, a story to enthrall friends with, only after it is survived.

While managing covert ops polygraph, I continued to conduct sensitive operational cases. In addition, I accompanied many experienced examiners on their first trip overseas. On these training trips, each examiner learned how to survive and operate in an overseas environment as I taught them how to safely polygraph and interrogate foreign agents. My contribution had direct and immediate impact on the quality of CIA operations overseas. The work was done using operational tradecraft to protect the agent, the case officer, and the facility used to conduct the test. Most important, it was employed to protect me. There were good reasons for the cases to be conducted clandestinely. The work was dangerous. The possibility of arrest, incarceration, and even death always existed. Cases were handled as secretly and inconspicuously as possible. Since my personality does not indulge in delusions of invulnerability, early on in my polygraph career I wisely decided that one of my goals in life should be to stay out of a foreign prison. That goal was indelibly etched on my mind much of the time I traveled overseas for the CIA. All prisons are terrible places to be, places to avoid at all cost, but a foreign prison is just about the last place on earth where anyone would want to be.

I found a home in the CIA's polygraph program and had a long career that offered an opportunity to see more of the world. The vast majority of the examinations I conducted overseas were routine, professionally planned, and well executed. Testing was successfully accomplished and everyone went home safely afterward. However, agent meetings intended to be surreptitious were sometimes planned without regard for sound tradecraft practices. Simple human error and unforeseen events endangered everyone despite careful planning. Several times my arrest on foreign soil seemed imminent. Covert ops cases that made my hair stand on end made operational polygraph seem so exciting to some polygraphers, but so dangerous to others. Some of my stories are humorous. Some are unbelievable. Some are frightening. All are true stories from my life as a cloak and dagger, spy vs. spy polygrapher.

Chapter Three

Destination:
Covert Ops Polygraph

He who cannot lie does not know what the
truth is.

—FRIEDRICH NIETZSCHE

Although I was an Agency Brat, I didn't decide to follow in my father's footsteps until after I graduated from college. I grew up around the world a dependent of a CIA officer. I had no grand plan to seek a career with the CIA, and I certainly never thought about security or polygraph work. My father did not encourage me to seek employment with the CIA, and it was never a goal of mine. Other than occasionally thinking about becoming a schoolteacher, I didn't develop any career goals until after graduating from college. I certainly enjoyed the life my father's career with the CIA provided, but I guess

I didn't realize that having my own career with the CIA would be the best way of ensuring that that way of life continued.

As an Agency Brat, my formative years were spent in countries around the world. My unusual childhood included numerous moves, losing good friends, making new ones, learning bits of several foreign languages, and attending many different schools. Prior to high school, I attended five different schools. I then attended seven different high schools in four years as a direct result of my father's assignments.

As a dependent overseas, I grew up living in off-base housing among the citizens of whatever country I was in at the time. As a young man overseas, I developed a burning curiosity about the world around me and always took advantage of any personal travel I could wrangle.

I've always been driven by an insatiable desire to see new places, and the desire did nothing but grow as time passed. During family road trips, while my brothers slept in the backseat of the car, my nose was glued to the window watching the scenery, buildings, and people we drove by. My desire to travel latched on to me like a burdensome mistress. What started as an itch to see what was on the other side of the hill developed into the need to travel the world to "see the elephant"—to see the wonders of the world for myself. Some people live their lives without traveling more than twenty miles from where they were born. Some are born fiddle-footed and have the urge to see what's on the other side of the hill. After they see what's there, they have to see what's on the other side of the next hill and then the next and the next. There's always something new and different to see.

By the time I reached college age, about half my life had been spent overseas. As a youngster, I traveled by train across the mountains of South America, swam in a river infested with jellyfish, was kidnapped in Uruguay, grew up in an English-speaking household with two German-speaking maids in a Spanish-speaking country, and traveled across the Pacific Ocean several times by ocean liner.

Thirteen years after World War II, I lived on Saipan, a tiny island in the Pacific Ocean. Saipan was once known as one of the Islas de los Ladrones (Thieves' Islands). Visiting Spanish ships in the 1800s apparently did not share the "what's mine is yours and what's yours is mine" philosophy of the Chamorro people they encountered. With their philosophy of community property, the Chamorro people saw nothing wrong in taking whatever they wanted from the Spanish ships. The Spanish, in contrast, considered it theft. Saipan is but a tiny speck in the ocean—about twelve miles long by five miles wide. Brutal fighting between Japanese and American soldiers during the twenty-four-day Battle of Saipan in 1944 resulted in a staggering death toll. Thirty thousand Japanese troops died in battle. Twenty-two thousand Japanese civilians on the island also perished. More than 3,000 American troops died, and 10,000 were wounded. Battleships, aircraft, artillery, and tanks caused the greatest number of casualties, but a great deal of the fighting was brutal hand-to-hand combat. Over and above the machine guns, rifles, pistols, and flamethrowers used during the battle, there was savage hand-to-hand fighting with bolo knives, bayonets, machetes, and swords. Two thousand American soldiers were killed during the first twenty-four hours of battle on the island (by way of comparison, about 5,800 American soldiers died in Iraq and Afghanistan during the first ten years of the War on Terror).

As a youngster, I camped in Saipan's jungles, swam in tropical lagoons, fished for barracuda and sand sharks, and climbed the island's mountains. I strolled along its tropical beaches and cut my way through its jungles with a machete. I traveled from island to island in the Pacific by small boat and found relics from gruesome World War II battles during "boondocking" excursions. My friends and I searched for war relics in the jungles of Saipan and regularly found bayonets, helmets, rifles, and stockpiles of ammunition. I used the gunpowder from old ammunition to build homemade rockets. I explored the rubble of bombed buildings and military command posts. I crawled into island caves, found skeletal remains of long-dead soldiers, and carried home human skulls (presumably Japanese). I cleaned the vegetation-and-vine-filled skulls in bleach and made them white once again. Over time, I managed to amass a small collection. It sounds quite morbid today, but when I was ten years old, it was "neat." I climbed over destroyed landing craft on the beaches, explored crashed aircraft on the sides of mountains, and played in rusted tanks in the jungles. I sat around campfires and listened to islanders' tales of the horrors of war. As a ten-year-old, I heard gruesome stories of the massive shelling of Saipan before the landing of American troops, accounts of fierce hand-to-hand fighting, and mind-numbing descriptions of thousands of civilians committing suicide in the last days of the battle. Many threw themselves to their deaths at Suicide Cliff and Banzai Cliff fearful of the approaching American soldiers.

Even my elementary school experiences were out of the ordinary. One of my schools was a Quonset hut. When I first learned the game of golf, nature's obstacles on the course consisted of gigantic coconut crabs and four-foot-long monitor lizards, not chipmunks and squirrels.

As a teenager, I traveled all over Japan by motorcycle and by train. I followed the Sumo wrestling championships instead of American football. I climbed to the top of Mount Fuji with a group of American servicemen and joined them as a student of Okinawan karate. I became a member of the Fuchu Motorcycle Club and traveled with club members to weekend races. I even entered a few races. The club members were daring servicemen, all around twenty-one to twenty-five years old. I had more in common with the servicemen than with others my age, so I did everything that a young serviceman who is stationed in the Far East would do even though I was only fifteen years old. There is no doubt that my atypical childhood is the source of my never-ending desire to see new places. From what I could tell from my friends in the United States, my childhood experiences were far different from theirs—different enough that their mouths would hang open when I recounted youthful adventures that must have sounded racy and rebellious, but was really just my daily life.

There are both positives and negatives in a childhood that is filled with frequent moves to new countries and new schools. On the positive side, I learned to be self-sufficient, self-reliant, and open to change. I learned to make new friendships. I developed an appreciation of world events, and learned to take a broad-minded look at events and appreciate the "big picture" rather than have a myopic, intolerant view of things. I believe living overseas and moving frequently created a breadth of experience in me that was unmatched by most teenagers.

On the other hand, in some ways I missed out on the normal "all-American boy" childhood that others experienced. I grew up very quickly in order to cope with all the change that was thrust upon me. I attained knowledge and experience usually reserved for others well beyond my years. I developed zero school spirit and had difficulty developing emotional attachments to specific places. My school spirit could have been contained in a thimble. To this day, I have trouble understanding the concept. Since I went to seven different high schools in four years due to my father's moves, school was just school to me. I could never understand why I should feel any special allegiance to any of them.

I attended Pennsylvania State University from 1966 through 1970 and that was the longest stretch of time I stayed in one spot through age twenty-two. My studies at Penn State were not designed to prepare me for a career with the CIA, certainly not as an interviewer, interrogator, and polygrapher for the CIA. In fact, I was somewhat of a lost soul during my college years. I had no career path in mind, and I had no idea what I wanted to do for a living. I changed majors four times. I went from education to psychology to anthropology, and ended up with a bachelor of arts degree in psychology.

After graduation, I was still not sure what I wanted to do with my life. I had four years of college under my belt, but I still had no specific job or career path in mind. I did very little interviewing with the companies that visited the campus during my senior year. My eventual decision to apply to the CIA actually resulted from discussions I had with my older brother. He had worked as a physical security officer in the Office of Security at the CIA for several years before he decided to return to college. When he talked to me about his former job, he described his various duties and responsibilities, as well as daily activities that included movement around Headquarters and travel to other buildings in the Washington DC area. To a wannabe world traveler who detested the idea of being desk bound at the age of twenty-two, his job sounded exciting. The more I mulled it over, the more appealing it sounded. I was still a lost soul regarding a long-term career, but my brother's former job sounded like it might be fun for a bit.

I interviewed with recruiters at the Agency's office in Northern Virginia, completed the application papers, and then waited months for the background investigation to be completed. I successfully completed an Entrance-on-Duty polygraph examination. This accomplishment was in no small part due to the skill and patience of the polygraph examiner assigned to my case (an examiner who was a true gentleman and who later became a colleague and friend). He sorted through my peccadilloes, listened to my tales of youthful indulgences, and put it all in proper perspective. It helped that I had managed to stay out of any serious trouble during my "atypical" childhood overseas, as well as in college. Finally, nearing the completion of CIA's processing hurdles, I entered on duty for the CIA in January 1971.

I found myself with a large group of young CIA officers, all at various stages of their quest for the top secret security clearance needed for employment with the CIA. We all entered on duty, despite the fact we were waiting for polygraph tests to be scheduled or background investigations to be completed, with the understanding that our employment could be terminated if we failed to successfully pass those security-processing requirements. We attended orientation training in a classroom in Northern Virginia. I was awaiting completion of my background investigation but had already undergone my polygraph examination. Although I did not lie during my examination, it was not a pleasant experience to be questioned on counterintelligence issues such as espionage, terrorism, revealing classified information, and secret contact with foreign nationals. There were also lifestyle issues such as committing serious crimes, using illegal drugs, engaging in homosexual activities, and falsifying personal history questionnaires. Some who returned from their examinations had attempted to lie to their polygraph examiners, usually to questions covering crimes and drugs. They told stories of being "unfairly" interrogated for hours. These stories of the torturous process circulated like wildfire among the others in the group who had yet to take their turn on "the box." During the training course, suspicion and trepidation about the polygraph process ran rampant throughout the group. Individuals received notification of their polygraph appointments during the course, and then after their time on "the box" at Headquarters, they would return to the classroom to await completion of other steps in their processing. With the successful completion of our security processing, we would depart for our new assignments.

Not everyone in the group survived processing. Some were called out of training a few days after their polygraph examination and did not return. There was never any official explanation. It was never announced that they didn't do well during their tests, but it was fairly obvious they were the latest victims of the "mental colonoscopy" known as the polygraph interview. Whenever the latest person was cut from the group, tension in the class soared and some could be seen squirming in their seats.

Our group was visited one day by an Agency security officer to discuss the nebulous topic of "Processing Issues." I suspect he was called in to squelch the group's fears of impending polygraph appointments. As he sauntered into the classroom with long, confident strides, two younger officers trailed behind him like puppy dogs. It was obvious to me they were there to learn from a master of his trade. Being tall, nattily dressed, and deep voiced, he was quite an impressive individual who bore some resemblance to the actor Sean Connery as he appeared in the early James Bond movies. Aside from his comportment, I was even more impressed with his composure in front of our group. He appeared to be completely at ease and totally in control. He was the type of individual who naturally commanded everyone's attention when he entered a room.

When the security officer spoke, everyone grew quiet and listened intently. It didn't take long for someone in the group to ask a question about an upcoming polygraph examination. My ears perked up when polygraph was mentioned, since I had recently completed my own polygraph examination and found it to be a rather extraordinary experience. The security officer spent a great deal of time on the topic of polygraph. It was obvious to me that the question from the audience allowed him to dwell on the real reason for his visit. In his response, he mentioned he was a former polygraph examiner. When he told our group he spent thirteen years conducting examinations as a polygraph examiner in the CIA's program, I was absolutely astonished. I must have stopped listening to him for a moment while my numbed mind tried to process his statement. Thirteen years. I reflected on all that my polygrapher had to do in a three-hour period to accomplish my examination. Thirteen years. As the enormity of a thirteen-year period of time sank in, I thought, *Thirteen years? My gosh! How could anyone do that type of work for thirteen years?*

One-and-a-half years later I entered the polygraph profession and tripled his thirteen-year assignment. I worked for him when he returned to the polygraph profession several years later as chief of the program. While there, he told me stories about his overseas experiences that made my hair curl. For instance, he was the only CIA polygraph examiner in history to have been shot while overseas. It may have only been a ricocheted bullet that hit him in the leg during a street crime, but he had been shot. Like many other examiners in the early years of the polygraph program, he spoke a foreign language. In fact, he didn't just speak one foreign language. He spoke German, French, Spanish, Japanese, and Chinese.

When all the steps of my security processing were completed, I finally left the orientation training course and started my new assignment as a physical security officer. It proved to be interesting, albeit short lived. It was an entry-level position in the world of security, but thanks to a despotic, sanctimonious supervisor, it also proved to be an unfortunate introduction to the world of employee-manager relations in the workplace. The position was exactly what I wanted and needed at the time, but I became jaded after a year. Also, I was newly married and definitely ready to move on to bigger and better things.

The job offered the variety it had promised; every day brought a variety of activities at Headquarters building, as well as at other buildings in the Washington DC area. The job mostly involved changing lock combinations and repairing safes and vaults, but after being weapons qualified, I also participated in the armed escort of money and classified materials around the city. As fun as it was, advancement opportunities were limited, and it simply was not the type of work I wanted to do for the duration of my CIA career. There were other assignments in the Office of Security that appeared to be equally as interesting, and they had excellent advancement opportunities. Fortunately, there was a personnel officer in the Office of Security who was familiar with my background, education, and current assignment. After discussing some possible reassignment options with me, he arranged for me to interview with Interrogation Research Section, as Polygraph Section was called in 1972.

The personnel officer orchestrated a meeting with Chief, Interrogation Research Section, the Section's highest ranking officer. The interview took place in the chief's office that was located on the right side of the main entrance of Headquarters building. It was a prime piece of office real estate. As I sat in his office during the interview, I was afforded a nice view through his windows of the circular drive at the entrance as well as the Headquarters auditorium; a bubble-like structure aptly nicknamed "The Bubble." The interview was rather lengthy, but I was pleased with how I responded to his inquiries and with what I learned from his responses to mine. I departed with the strong sense that I had favorably impressed the chief, and I walked away with a better understanding of the Section and a strong desire to give polygraph work a try. Prior to the interview, I had done my homework by finding out what I could about the Agency's polygraph program, and I talked with both my father and older brother, both of whom had also undergone polygraph examinations for the Agency.

At the end of the interview, I asked permission to return with follow-up questions. He seemed impressed with my request, probably because he was trying to determine whether I had the traits of a natural investigator—someone who was thorough, detailed, and analytical. While he assessed me during the interview, I did my best to assess him, also. It did not escape me that the chief seemed to place a lot of emphasis on the side of the polygraph profession that supported the Agency's overseas operations, and he stressed that I would be required to undertake a good deal of foreign travel. Away from the pressure of the interview, I thought of follow-up questions to ask about what I could expect from an assignment to the Section. I wanted to know what a typical day in the Section would be like for me, where foreign and domestic trips would take me, how long typical trips would be, and how many trips I would be taking each year. I also wanted to know what the polygraph examiner training course would entail.

My second interview with the chief was held several days later, and once again I found myself in his office sitting in front of his huge wood desk with the spectacular view of the Agency's entrance and the auditorium. During the second interview, I bombarded him with questions. I believe the sheer volume and depth of questions I asked impressed him, particularly since I concentrated on the overseas operations side of the job, as he had done during our previous meeting. As the interview came to a close, I asked if he could arrange for me to speak with someone else in the Section. He introduced me to the Section's training officer, a crusty old gentleman with more wrinkles on his face than a topographical map drawn by three drunken men on a ship being tossed around by a tropical storm. Sometime later, I heard it said that there was a wrinkle on his face for every liar he ever encountered. I must have left a favorable impression with the wrinkled training officer as well, because, despite my relative youth, I was subsequently offered the assignment to Interrogation Research Section.

Although there is no doubt that a childhood filled with foreign travel made me attractive to Polygraph Section management when I interviewed with them at the young age of twenty-three, my acceptance by the two older gentlemen was actually quite extraordinary. The Section was manned by only a handful of examiners at Headquarters. I was quite a bit younger than most of the examiners. Each seemed to have decades of security and operations experience and several were approaching retirement age. The younger examiners who were closest to my age were all around ten years older than I. I later found out that my first day in the Section was one day too late to see the Section Chief, the training officer, and two other examiners, since they had retired the Friday before I reported for duty to the office. Up to that point in time, I was the youngest officer to ever enter the Agency's polygraph program, a silly record I was to hold for about the next twenty years.

During my first days on the job, I learned that covert

operations polygraph testing was the most sought after assignment in the Interrogation Research Section. About one-fourth of the Section's total number of examiner positions were overseas positions. Actually, in 1972 the Section was a small-scale operation compared to the program today. Many of the examiners in the Section spoke a second language, and many of them were positioning themselves to compete for future overseas assignments. Whenever a desirable overseas position became available, it was said in a half-joking manner that there would be blood on the walls before the selection was made. Examiners actually got angry at their coworkers for applying for a position because it lessened their chance of getting the assignment. The grind of conducting applicant and reinvestigation cases every day at Headquarters was nowhere near as desirable as traveling the world to conduct much more fulfilling and interesting operations cases.

After completing polygraph training, I started conducting cases on a daily basis under the guidance of the training officer. I knew that he was satisfied with my performance and that the cases I completed were well done, but I couldn't shake the nagging feeling that I was actually ill prepared. I felt that I could, and should, be doing the job even better. I knew that the future would bring cases of much greater complexity.

During my training, it was constantly stressed that the CIA considered the polygraph process to be an aid to interrogation. My training officer stressed that my mission was to obtain any reportable information regarding the issues under investigation and report the information to the adjudicators. Interrogation and the reporting of information obtained during polygraph examinations were stressed much more than the technical results of actual polygraph testing. Unlike today, polygraph reports made no mention of the Deception Indicated, No Deception Indicated, or Inconclusive results of testing. Final reports contained information provided by or elicited from the subject during the polygraph session. This information was categorized as Favorable (no reportable information was obtained), Unfavorable (information was obtained that was previously unknown and that would have impact on the adjudication), or Derogatory (significant information was obtained that could lead to the denial of a security clearance when adjudicated).

I realized that I should become as knowledgeable and as skilled as possible in the art of interrogation in order to be truly effective and successful on the job. I felt the instruction I received during the basic polygraph examiner training course didn't provide the tools I needed to conduct consistently successful interrogations. It was clear to me that the path to improvement and greater success could only be achieved through self-study.

My first order of business on the road to self-improvement through self-study was to check out every book on interrogation I could find in the CIA library. I also talked with my fellow examiners. Many had excellent reputations and appeared to be quite skilled and knowledgeable. I frequently engaged them in conversation regarding polygraph cases and interrogations around the world. I listened, learned, and tucked many of their tactics into my interrogation tool bag. There was one well-respected examiner who volunteered a significant amount of time teaching me about the world of polygraph in support of covert operations. Each time his polygraph charts, notes, and draft reports from his most recent overseas trip arrived at Headquarters, he called me to his office and reviewed each case with me. He described the background of each case and the arrangements made to conduct the test. He then reviewed the polygraph charts obtained and described interrogations he conducted. I learned a great deal from him. I also became quite envious as he recounted his tales of cases conducted in exotic lands around the world. I wanted to be like him. I wanted to travel the world.

Chapter Four

On the Road

A lie can travel half way around the world
while the truth is still putting on its shoes.
— MARK TWAIN

After one year of conducting various types of examinations at Headquarters, I was selected to go on my first trip overseas to conduct covert operations cases. An examiner's first trip was called a "training trip" by the office because he was accompanied by a senior examiner who taught him how to conduct cases in foreign environments under vastly different conditions from those at Headquarters. During my first year, several CIA courses introduced me to the fundamentals of the Directorate of Operations' (now known as the National Clandestine Service) work overseas: surveillance, counter surveillance, agent meetings, cover, agent validation techniques, etc. I had also conducted several covert cases in the Washington DC area, at first under the guidance of a senior examiner.

During my first year in the Section, I had formed my own opinions about the strengths and weaknesses of the other examiners. Duke, the senior examiner chosen to accompany me on my training trip, was a likable fellow. I felt he was clearly one of the most competent and most likable of the bunch, and I held him in very high regard. Duke was the type of man who was the last one to quit work at the end of the day and the first one to buy the beer. If you bought him a beer instead, he would tell you polygraph stories guaranteed to delight and enthrall. If you bought him two beers, the stories might even be true. He had been in the Section long enough to have several overseas tours and numerous overseas TDY (Temporary Duty) assignments under his belt. He was well educated, witty, and had a wealth of both life and polygraph experience that gave him perspective and knowledge.

Equally as important, I felt Duke was an examiner with integrity and a strong sense of fair play—important qualities, I believe, for a polygraph examiner. I have only befriended a handful of individuals during my career whom I admired, respected, and above all, trusted—"battle buddies," as they are called in the military. Duke became such a trusted friend for me. I didn't know it at the time, but our five-week partnership was the beginning of a friendship that has lasted for decades.

He was an accomplished and effective interrogator, a world traveler, and a devotee of fine food and wine. He had a good sense of humor and facetiously referred to himself as a "Counterspy Extraordinaire." Even though he had the audacity to refer to me as "Preppy," a moniker he still uses to this day, I was actually very fortunate to have him as my training trip instructor. I could not have personally selected any better examiner or training trip partner for my first TDY.

Prior to my training trip, what I knew about operating as an overseas covert operations polygraph examiner could have fit in a shot glass with room left over for a healthy swig of whiskey. My first TDY overseas was a five-week-long opportunity to learn the ropes from a highly experienced examiner. Duke shared survival tips, the fine points of international travel, and how to live and operate on a daily basis in foreign environments. With regard to the duties and responsibilities of a traveling examiner, he taught me how to deal with office personnel, how to write reports, how to send our materials back to the home office, and how to properly use interpreters during the conduct of polygraph examinations. Above all else, he doggedly emphasized the importance of secure arrangements for the conduct of our polygraph examinations. He had been in the polygraph business a lot longer than I and told many stories about times he feared he might be arrested. I listened and I learned. His chilling stories caused me to pause and reflect. I began to worry about what I had gotten myself into as I was about to begin conducting intelligence activities on be-half of the CIA on foreign soil.

During the time we spent together preparing for the extended TDY, Duke entertained me with stories about compromised agents, operations gone bad, and CIA offi-cers incarcerated in foreign prisons. One story in particu-lar left an impression on me.

In the early days of the CIA, two CIA officers flew low over a communist country attempting to extract one of their agents. Two contract pilots and the two CIA officers planned to lift the agent off the ground by means of an aer-ial snatch. In order to accomplish this difficult task, the agent would sit on the ground wearing a harness attached to a wire suspended high overhead. The low-flying airplane would hook the agent and haul him aboard as the airplane gained speed and altitude to quickly depart the area.

Unknown to the four men on the airplane, their entire team of agents had been captured by the country's intelli-gence and security forces soon after they had entered the country. They told their captors everything about their mis-sion and their CIA trainers and handlers. They had been "turned" by their captors and revealed everything about their mission and the planned extraction of the one team member by an aerial hook from a low-flying aircraft. The four men on the airplane flew straight into a trap.

The airplane arrived at the pickup site according to schedule and all seemed to be proceeding as planned as it made its first pass over the site. The appropriate recogni-tion signals were seen on the ground and final preparations were made to affect the snatch. As the slow, low-flying approach was made, camouflaged antiaircraft guns opened fire on the airplane. The airplane was struck by rounds shot from both sides, crashed into the trees, broke apart, and burst into flames. Despite the severity of the crash, the two CIA officers survived, although both pilots died. Communist security forces captured the two officers as they stood beside the flaming wreckage. They were injured, but they were alive.

The two officers were grabbed, tied up, and taken to jail cells in a nearby town. They were eventually transferred to a prison located hundreds of miles away, placed in separate cells, and kept in chains.

Back in the United States, the CIA had absolutely no information on the fate of the missing airplane and presumed that all four men on board were dead. The families of the four were eventually notified of that presumption. The death of the two pilots and the status of the two live Agency officers were known only to the intelligence and security forces of the communist country.

The two officers were kept totally separated in captivity and did not see each other for the first two years of their confinement. During that time, they suffered through lengthy interrogation sessions and were subjected to sleep deprivation tactics. They were also terrorized with threats of torture and execution.

Two years after they were captured, the two prisoners finally saw each other for the first time. Unfortunately, their reunion was not a happy one. It was at their trial. They were convicted of espionage. One received a sentence of twenty years, and the other received a sentence of life in prison. The Agency first learned that the two officers were still alive when the communist country publicly announced the two had been convicted as spies for the CIA and were currently in prison serving their sentences.

The CIA tried for years to bring about their release, but all diplomatic efforts proved to be futile. Diplomatic relations with the country involved finally improved in 1971, and the first of the officers was released. He had spent nineteen years of his life in prison. The second officer was released in 1973 after spending over twenty years of his life in prison. Both could attribute their incarcerations to a compromised agent, one whose loyalty has been turned to the opposition. When I listened to this story, it didn't escape me that I was soon going to be traveling to foreign countries to meet with agents that might be compromised. In fact, it was going to be my job to help determine whether or not that was the case.

Duke told me this story only several weeks before our departure to South America. It gave me a lot to think about as I was preparing to be thrust into the world of overseas covert operations. The two officers were about my age when they were captured, interrogated, tried on espionage charges, and imprisoned. The story was also very recent, since the second officer had been released only about a year before the story was recounted to me. It clearly exemplified that espionage was not a gentlemen's game and that operational security issues were of prime importance in the conduct of operations overseas. The story drove home the point that a covert operation that goes bad can result in loss of freedom or life.

As if he hadn't given me enough to think about, my traveling companion continued raising the hairs on the back of my neck by relating yet another story of a CIA officer who had been arrested while working in a foreign country. I'll call the officer Larry. Not only was Larry arrested, he was incarcerated for a very long time in a foreign prison, the kind of place I had already decided to avoid at all cost.

My partner recounted the story of a fateful interview of an agent conducted by Larry, a debriefer and linguist who spoke the agent's language fluently. Larry's extended TDY took him to several other countries before arriving at the capital city of the agent's country. He had visited there many times before, and in fact, was requested by name because he spoke the language fluently. Larry was scheduled to conduct an interview of an agent who had been recently recruited as a penetration of the local government. With Larry's help, the office wanted to establish the agent's bona fides, the veracity of his reporting, and the security of the secret working relationship. Larry met with a case officer from the local office as well with a TDY case officer who had previously met the agent and was responsible for securing the man's agreement to work for American intelligence. On the day of the interview, they gathered in the apartment that was going to be used as the meeting site that evening. During their meeting, they discussed the agent's background and the history of his contact with American intelligence officers. They agreed upon questions to ask during the interview and settled on the meeting arrangements. Larry was given the keys to the apartment at the conclusion of the meeting. That evening the TDY case officer and Larry would meet with the agent while the local case officer would remain at his office.

Larry was the first to arrive at the apartment that evening. About thirty minutes later, the TDY case officer arrived with the agent. Immediately upon being introduced to the agent, Larry made note of his obvious anxiety. All newly recruited agents beginning a clandestine relationship with a foreign intelligence service are nervous. An experienced interviewer will note a degree of anxiety that is clearly out of the ordinary. The nervousness encountered by Larry that evening developed into a level he thought was clearly out of the ordinary.

The interview didn't progress very far. The agent's nervous interaction with two American intelligence officers escalated into outright agitation over the situation he found himself in. His anxiety reached higher levels of intensity as he expressed discomfort and regret, not only about the meeting that evening, but also about his initial agreement to enter into a secret relationship with the Americans. He complained about being asked to produce classified documents and expressed regret at previously signing a contract to work for the United States. He demanded the immediate return of the contract, desperately wanting to have it in his hands so he could tear it to shreds. The agent also raised the topic the debriefer thought was the real reason for his agitation—the invasive nature of the interview. He wanted the interview to end and expressed distrust over the motivations of the American intelligence officers. Larry did his best to overcome the agent's objections but was unable to persuade him to continue the interview. He did manage to secure the agent's agreement to reflect on his decision and meet with them again the following night if he changed his mind.

Larry and the TDY case officer were very concerned with the agent's unexpected behavior and attitude. The excessive nervousness and desire to terminate the relationship came as a total surprise. The case officer escorted the agent out of the apartment. Now alone in the apartment, Larry placed the interview questions and notes in an envelope to be transported back to the office. He then telephoned the case officer at the local office to advise that the interview had been cut short. The case officer asked Larry to be ready to depart in thirty minutes, the length of time it would take him to travel to the apartment.

When the case officer arrived at the apartment, Larry grabbed the envelope containing his questions and notes, as well as a bottle of beer from the refrigerator. They went straight down to the entrance of the apartment building and headed for the case officer's car parked in the apartment building courtyard.

As they glanced to the right and to the left, they noticed a half dozen men dressed in brown suits quickly converging on them. They ran to the car. The envelope with the incriminating material was tossed onto the backseat.

Before they could drive away, a man approached the car and yelled at them to stop. Ignoring the pursuer's command, the case officer gripped the steering wheel tightly, stomped on the accelerator, and maneuvered his now speeding car around a car that barricaded the road. A high-speed car chase ensued through the streets of the city with two cars trailing close behind them. Although there was little chance of a successful escape, the case officer raced through the city streets at high speed. Larry looked out the rear window and saw two vehicles following close behind. His thoughts turned to the destruction of the incriminating questions and notes from the interview session. He decided to destroy the evidence by eating it. After shredding the paper with his hands, he found that fear and adrenaline effectively put a stop to his normal saliva production. He couldn't swallow the shredded paper with a mouth as dry as a cat's litter box. Remembering the beer that he took from the apartment's refrigerator, he tried soaking the shredded paper with beer but found the process to be too time consuming. Time was short, as the two cars were very close behind. While the car was still racing through the streets, he decided to toss the paper out the car window as fast as he could shred it.

Their luck ran out as the case officer's car finally approached an intersection at the wrong time. The stoplight was red, and their escape route was blocked by cars in all lanes. The men in brown suits quickly surrounded them with guns drawn and put an end to their attempted escape. Both men were ordered out of the car, handcuffed, arrested, and taken away to jail. At the time of his arrest, Larry still had a list of interview questions in his coat pocket.

Both men were interrogated by government officials for days. It is said that the case officer rather quickly admitted he was CIA and was released. Larry followed instructions for such situations and stuck to his cover story. He wasn't released. Also, he wasn't allowed to contact the American Embassy for many days. When he was finally allowed to meet with an embassy official, the man offered little help and less hope.

Larry tried to settle into the daily routine of life in prison but became emotionally distressed by an event he witnessed daily outside his prison bars. Every day at lunchtime, the guards ate while sitting on stools near his cell. All of the guards had wicked-looking, large knives with curved blades on their belts. When a guard ate fruit with his lunch, he unsheathed his knife, peeled the fruit, deliberately sliced his finger until blood flowed, and then resheathed the knife. They may have been voluntarily following the code found in a phrase engraved on Spanish swords for many years, "Do not draw me without reason. Do not sheath me without honor." More likely, they were following orders to draw blood if their weapons left their sheaths. The guards were clearly tough as nails, no-nonsense types who took their job seriously enough to follow their orders to the letter. Their willingness to bloody themselves in such a fashion put a damper on any thoughts Larry had of attempting an escape.

Larry didn't know it at the time, but the U.S. government was engaged in behind-the-scenes negotiations for his release. It was rumored that the negotiations involved an offer of a large cash payment. However, Larry remained incarcerated for a very long time. On the day Larry was ordered out of his cell by a few somber, sour-faced officials, he believed his captors were taking him out to be shot in the back of the head and put to bed with a pick and a shovel for a long dirt nap. He reluctantly left his cell, but his will to survive screamed for him to stay right where he was instead of being marched off to his death. The trauma of that experience far outweighed the joy that eventually set in when he finally realized he was truly being released.

Duke's stories, more than any other story or any other piece of information I gleaned from training courses, hammered home the importance of his constant vigilance over operational security issues. They illustrated quite clearly that the threat of arrest and incarceration was real and that the gentlemen's game of espionage was really an extremely serious enterprise.

Given that I was a young polygraph examiner making preparations to embark on my first journey to foreign countries to conduct covert operations cases for the Directorate of Operations, when I heard this story I paused for some serious reflection on my choice of careers. I was young and therefore did not have a great fear of my own mortality, but I was smart enough to realize that the conduct of covert cases overseas posed a threat to my freedom and perhaps even my life. Woody Allen and I feel the same way about death. He once said, "I'm not afraid of dying. I just don't want to be there when it happens." I decided it would be extremely prudent to listen carefully to Duke. His constant vigilance over operational security issues rose to a new level of relevance. I knew that prisons could be absolutely terrible places and that conditions in foreign prisons could be horrendous. I decided that staying out of prison should be one of my goals in life. In addition, some time had passed since Larry had been arrested, world politics had changed, and the CIA had become a large bureaucratic organization. I wasn't working in my father's CIA. I had little faith in the U.S. government's desire or ability to get my fanny out of a foreign jail, and I simply couldn't conceive of the government paying large sums of money for my release. I decided I had better look out for my own safety as best I could.

The trip with Duke was a constant, day and night flurry of activity involving taxis, hotels, airports, CIA offices, and safe houses. We conducted thirty-five cases during five weeks of work in seven major cities in South America. Our visit to the continent did not go unnoticed by foreign intelligence services. I detected foot surveillance in one city when we went shopping one day after we left the office. I saw a man's reflection in store windows at least four times during our mile-long walk down a shopping street. Fortunately, we were not on our way to conduct a covert case at the time.

In another city, the office was extremely ill prepared for our visit. We had a large number of cases to conduct but were unable to get any of them accomplished during the first several days we were there. No one at the office was in charge of the scheduling of cases, and the case officers were unavailable for consultation. We even had difficulty getting our hands on the files we needed to review to prepare for the cases. My partner was riled up enough to chew nails and spit out thumbtacks. We met with the Deputy Chief to try and get some order restored. Prior to the meeting, I tried to warn my partner to approach him with tact and diplomacy.

"Alan," he said. "I'm a graduate of the Will Rogers School of Diplomacy."

"What's that?" I replied.

He explained: "Will Rogers said that diplomacy is the art of saying 'Nice doggie' until you can find a rock."

The night before our meeting with the Deputy Chief, we saw *Walking Tall*, a movie about Sheriff Buford Pusser who battled his town's gambling, prostitution, and bootlegging problems. The sheriff stood up against the town's rotten elements with a four-foot long oak club. With the next day's meeting on our minds, both of us released a lot of tension while watching Sheriff Pusser bash the heads of the bad guys with his big club. We exited the movie theater having received the movie's message that when you know what is right, you shouldn't be afraid to stand up for it. As much as he may have wanted to, my partner was unable to carry a four-foot long oak club to the office the next day. Nevertheless, I am sure that Buford Pusser's example provided him with inspiration, self-righteous determination, and intestinal fortitude he needed. During our meeting with the Deputy Chief, I watched as my training trip partner skillfully used persuasive arguments, dramatics, and an ultimatum in order to ensure our needs were met. My partner's view of diplomacy spoke volumes. In my comparative youth, I sometimes considered his views on such matters to be rather intolerant. However, as I matured I found myself following in his intolerant footsteps and searching for a rock more and more frequently. With age comes wisdom.

In another South American city, a case officer served as interpreter while I examined his agent. Unfortunately, he could not properly read test questions that had been written down in Spanish for him by the chief of the office. Since I determined he was much more of a hindrance than a help, I had no choice but to unceremoniously expel him from the room. I took on the job of interpreter myself, since my limited grasp of the language was far superior to his.

On another stop, we had not been properly briefed on the after-hours entry procedure for the office. Attempting to meet with a case officer at the office one night, we found a complicated array of buttons that operated buzzers and intercom systems at the entrance to the building. We mistakenly pushed the buzzer or alarm system button while trying to speak into the intercom. The guard on duty inside watched our shenanigans on closed-circuit TV. Although unable to hear us, he finally decided to buzz the door open when he realized we couldn't operate the electronic panel outside. We entered the lobby. As I headed toward the guard desk, I reached into the inside pocket of my overcoat to pull out my passport for identification. I didn't realize it at the time, but it looked like I was reaching for a gun. As my eyes moved from my coat pocket to the guard desk, I saw the guard standing behind his desk taking aim at my chest with a shotgun. Dying by friendly fire wasn't one of my concerns when I left the United States, but that night, that possibility stared me straight in the face.

I was asked to polygraph the office's penetration of a terrorist organization at one of our stops. The agent had recently reported to his case officer that his organization was going to start randomly assassinating Americans on the streets of the city. When the agent's information of planned assassinations of Americans was passed to Headquarters, it caused quite a commotion. Headquarters wanted the information verified through polygraph testing before it was further disseminated throughout the Intelligence Community.

When Duke heard the case involved terrorists and assassination plots, he thought his time would be better spent in the hotel bar while I, the junior examiner, conducted the case on the other side of the city. I should probably claim that he assigned the case to the better examiner, but somehow I don't believe that was his reasoning or motivation for assigning the case to me.

Actually, this story doesn't involve the application of a lengthy, skilled interrogation on my part. As happens with some cases, significant information was elicited during routine pretest discussion. An elemental part of a polygraph interview is a thorough discussion with the examinee of the issues to be covered during polygraph testing.

During the pretest I said, "So, I understand you told us your organization is going to start randomly assassinating Americans on the streets of the city."

"No. That is not correct," he replied.

It didn't take a trained interrogator to realize that something wasn't right. To make certain, I continued, "Now wait a minute. During your last meeting with Bill [the case officer], you reported to him that you attended your organization's meeting recently. At that meeting they said they were going to start random assassinations. Isn't that correct?"

"No," he replied. "At that meeting the idea of random assassinations was discussed. It was only discussed. There was a lot of talk and a lot of anger expressed, but there was no decision to randomly assassinate Americans. Actually, it was set aside as a bad idea."

Well, obviously there had been a miscommunication somewhere. Erroneous information had been reported to Headquarters and a lot of people had been needlessly alarmed. Considering that I was going to be an American roaming the streets of the city for another week, I was happy that a mistake had been made. Duke, who had waited out my polygraph interview in a bar on the other side of the city, was also happy with the test results.

Thanks to Duke, I had what many described as a "meteoric" career in the Office of Security. My strengths and abilities were recognized early on, I successfully handled assignments of increasing responsibility, and I was promoted rapidly. Duke was responsible for that early recognition, and other than my own drive to succeed and perform well, I thankfully attribute the beginning of my rapid rise to him. His unsolicited support began shortly after the completion of my training trip when he was promoted to a management position in the Section. He was responsible for overseeing the daily operation of all cases conducted at Headquarters, including the occasional conduct of tests on Agency employees suspected of wrongdoing. One such case involving a senior Agency employee was dumped on the Section Chief's shoulders by the Director of Security not long after our trip. When the chief conferred with Duke regarding the case, he suggested that a senior, highly experienced examiner be assigned to it. Duke recommended me, even though I was the youngest examiner in the Section. There were examiners in the Section who were five grades higher with more than a decade of experience. Duke explained that he just spent five weeks on the road in South America watching me conduct difficult covert operational cases and deal with senior Agency personnel. He thought I would do the best job.

As a result of his unwavering support, I conducted the case, no doubt while being nervously monitored by the chief. Duke's kind words and support were clearly responsible for my early recognition. I never forgot what he did. In fact, I followed his example and did the same for deserving young officers throughout the years.

During my career in polygraph, I accompanied many examiners on their training trips. The trips were typically whirlwind affairs involving travel to about six countries in as many weeks. They involved a great deal of travel in and out of airports, hotels, and Agency offices. There was frequent night work as well as work on most Saturdays. Sundays were usually good days to travel on to the next country. Back in 1973, introducing an examiner to the world of covert operations polygraph was an on-the-job, one-on-one proposition with a senior examiner. There was no formal operational polygraph course until the mid-1980s when I took charge of polygraph training.

By the end of my first two years in the Section, I had hands-on experience with a wide variety of applicant, contractor, reinvestigation, and specific issue tests on employees under investigation for suspected wrongdoing. I had taken several domestic trips and also handled the grandest type of case—the covert operations case. I had conducted many covert operations cases in the local Washington DC area, traveled on a five-week swing of South American countries with a training trip instructor, and completed several foreign trips by myself. Much of my life up to that time had already been spent overseas as a dependent, and I thoroughly enjoyed the opportunity the Interrogation Research Section gave me to see many new cities and I was by far the youngest examiner in the Section and had the lowest grade. At that time, I was four grades lower than the journeyman grade level. On the other hand, I knew that I had a solid reputation as an examiner. I make no claims of being the best or the most successful examiner in the Section. I continued my polygraph education by studying those I considered to be the best of the best. I had my own share of successful cases working side by side with the Section's group of seasoned examiners, and I even outperformed a few who were senior to me in both grade and experience. Thankfully, my work didn't go unnoticed. There were several Section managers who kept assigning me to cases of increasing complexity—I'm sure to put me to the test. I took it as a challenge. I enjoyed my work, and I enjoyed being in a profession composed of worldly, seasoned, and skilled polygraph examiners. My fellow examiners were accomplished interviewers and interrogators, and I was part of it all. I felt that the work was vitally important and that we were the most skillful and highly trained people in the entire world in a small, unique profession. To put it simply, it was fun, rewarding, and worthwhile. I was fortunate that some of my managers recognized my abilities. Don't misunderstand me. The Section was far from anyone's vision of a workplace utopia. It was just like any other office in any other profession. We all experienced our share of bad days, frustrations, missed promotions, lost assignments, bad supervisors, and lousy work environments. That being said, I found a home. I enjoyed my job, and I realized I wanted to specialize in the elite covert operations testing. It was my favorite category of testing, especially if it involved the opportunity to travel to foreign countries. There were quite a few countries in the world I had yet to visit.

Chapter Five

Trying Times

No man has a good enough memory to be a
successful liar.

—ABRAHAM LINCOLN

L
ike every young person new to a career, I
was ambitious and worked very hard to make a
name for myself. Being the youngest man in polygraph didn't make that goal any easier. Craving the excitement of foreign travel, I sought an overseas PCS (Permanent
Change of Station) assignment. I expressed interest in a
June 1975 assignment to Vietnam, a war zone. A tour in
Saigon would expose me to different types of covert operations cases in the city, as well as offer the opportunity
to handle cases throughout the country. A government car
would be made available for my use, and I would be housed

in the city. Any travel out of the city would be accomplished by a U.S. Army helicopter. Also, I would receive a pay differential in addition to danger pay. The assignment sounded like a fantastic opportunity to get on my feet financially while experiencing overseas living in an exotic, albeit war-torn Asian country. The city of Saigon was relatively safe at that time and since it was considered to be a family post, my wife could accompany me. I was ecstatic when I was finally informed that I had been officially selected by the Office of Security Career Board to replace the returning examiner.

In the months before our departure, I went through all the normal steps to make the move from Washington to Saigon. Arrangements were made to put most of our household effects into storage, while a large shipment of our personal belongings was sent to Saigon in advance of our departure. Our house was listed to rent, and I turned my attention to trying to dispose of our two personal automobiles. I quickly sold one of them. My wife and I underwent routine medical and psychiatric tests required by the Office of Medical Services. We also received a multitude of inoculations, including plague, yellow fever, and rabies.

In the midst of our processing for the move, the Saigon office made a surprise request. I was asked to depart months ahead of schedule in order to assist with the increasing polygraph workload and to overlap with the departing examiner. I agreed. So, in March 1975 my wife and I hurriedly departed Washington DC. Our real estate

company had not yet found renters for our house. Unable
to get a good sale price before our rushed departure, our
remaining automobile was sold at the last minute at a great
loss. Nevertheless, we were on our way and soon arrived in
Honolulu, exhausted as everyone always is who attempts
such moves. My wife and I planned a short vacation there
before continuing on our trip. Initially, we had a magnifi-
cent time in Honolulu, but we listened carefully to the
news every evening and soon heard that conditions in Saigon were rapidly deteriorating. Troops were advancing on
the city. Wives of American Embassy employees were being flown out of the country. Saigon was fast becoming a
place that was not safe enough to be considered a family
post and its future was questionable. Increasingly worried,
I wasn't very surprised when I received a phone call from
Headquarters at 4:30 A.M. on our fourth night there. I was
ordered to return.

We contacted relatives, had our airline tickets rewrit-
ten, and then returned home. My parents graciously accepted us as houseguests. My assignment was put on hold
for the next six weeks until Saigon fell to the advancing
communists on April 30, 1975. With my assignment to Saigon officially canceled, I quickly trotted into the Chief of
Polygraph Section's office.

"I have an arm full of shots, I'm living out of a suitcase, all my belongings are in Saigon or in storage, I have
no cars, and my house is empty," I said. "Please send me
somewhere! I'll go anywhere!"

I knew there was no vacant position for an overseas

polygraph examiner anywhere else in the world at that time. My only hope was the million-to-one chance that he might push for the creation of an extra position in one of our other overseas locations, but he was unable to help.

The Agency amended my travel orders from a Permanent Change of Station (PCS) move to Saigon to a Temporary Duty trip to Honolulu and return. Declaring that I technically never set foot outside the United States, they insisted I pay back all the money advanced to me, money I no longer had. Continuing with our streak of bad luck, my wife and I discovered our household effects were being held hostage by striking union workers. We couldn't get our household effects out of storage. We found ourselves having to continue imposing on my parents for a place to stay, we were unable to move back into our house, we had to replace two automobiles, and we owed the Agency a lot of money. Making the situation even worse, we learned our shipment of household effects sent to Saigon ahead of our departure was lost forever after being seized by the Viet Cong. Our first attempted PCS was a fiasco but, if nothing else, it makes for a good story.

I submitted a claim for the lost shipment. The value of every item in the shipment was depreciated. I was reimbursed a fraction of the items' original cost. The shipment also contained all the photographs and slides I had taken on TDYs to Central and South America. There was absolutely no way I could replace them.

Time passed and my continuing quest for an overseas assignment was finally fulfilled. In 1976, my wife, our infant daughter, Lisa, and I began a tour in the Far East. Although my first attempt at a PCS was a trying time, my three years in the Far East were absolutely fascinating. The centuries-old customs, cultures, and languages were intriguing. Perhaps I was influenced by spending part of my childhood in Japan, but I felt a particular attraction to everything Asian. The languages in the Far East are not romance languages and are much more difficult than the Spanish I studied earlier in my career.

When I started with Polygraph Section in 1972, pairs of examiners routinely took swings through Central and South America to handle many cases for the Agency's overseas offices. My very first assignment was to take a full-time, six-month-long Spanish language training course. Full-time language training was intense. It involved one topic, eight hours a day, five days a week for six months. In addition to the eight-hour days with the instructors, I had homework every night and weekend and listened to audiotapes to memorize dialogues in Spanish during my daily commutes.

I was placed in a class that had started months before my arrival. It sounded to me as if they were already speaking Spanish fluently. The training was rigorous and I constantly struggled because my classmates were always ahead of me. One by one they dropped out of training to move on to their overseas assignments. By the end of the six months, I was left all alone with a series of instructors who took turns during my eight-hour day.

At the end of training, I was scheduled to take a fluency test to determine what level I had attained in reading, speaking, and comprehension. The test to evaluate my speaking ability was the one that worried me the most. It involved speaking with two instructors for about a half hour. They would control the flow of the conversation to make sure it became progressively more complicated.

On the day of the oral examination, I entered the room and saw that two of my former instructors were going to evaluate me. I liked them very much and knew they would be as fair as possible, but I also realized they knew my strengths and weaknesses better than anyone. Nevertheless, before they had time to get beyond the initial greetings, I started talking. I talked for what seemed like an eternity and saw expressions of both surprise and approval register on the faces of the two instructors. They stopped me from time to time to ask questions, and fortunately, I was able to provide answers. I managed to consume a hefty portion of the thirty minutes allotted for the oral test. My rapid-fire oral onslaught for a full fifteen minutes boosted my confidence enough to enable me to speak fairly well during the rest of the session. The session did become more complicated, but I left feeling satisfied with my performance and quite confident that I simply couldn't have performed any better.

When I received the results of my evaluation several days later I was delightfully surprised. I received a Level Three in speaking. A person who attained a Level Four was considered to be fluent. One of the instructors told me she was extremely impressed with the way I enthusiastically entered the exam room and talked with such animation and excitement. She said the language school realized what a difficult time I had during training by being placed in an advanced class. She said I deserved the high evaluation. More good news followed. My office recommended me for a language achievement award, and I eventually received a certificate and a check for $1,000. To put a $1,000 amount in the perspective it deserves, I should mention I started at the Agency two years earlier in 1971 with a pitifully miniscule annual salary of $6,950. An award of $1,000 was actually an enormous amount for me. Sometimes with great struggle comes great reward.

Struggle, conflict, and trying times are probably encountered by almost everyone during their careers. I seemed to have my fair share as a polygraph manager. However, one memorable conflict with another federal agency in the 1990s actually contributed to my notoriety in the profession. As a result of that interagency conflict, I can claim more examinations attributable to me than any CIA polygraph examiner in history. A former CIA polygrapher who is a friend of mine actually made a similar claim several years ago. However, I can produce indisputable evidence in the form of U.S. government records to prove that I conducted more examinations than any other CIA polygraph examiner in history. Actually, the number of cases my friend conducted pales in comparison to those attributed to me.

In the early 1990s, another federal agency established

its own polygraph program with field offices located throughout the United States. Before that, they received test results from examinations of joint interest conducted by the CIA. Even after the new program became operational, the CIA continued its support. As the program manager in Polygraph Section, I was responsible for providing that support.

When the other agency requested that we input all of our case data into their new computer system, Polygraph Section initially declined. The other agency was insistent and argued that our participation in their new record keeping system was vital. They were resolute and unyielding in their demands. We were adamant in our refusal to input our data into their new system. Of particular concern was the identity of our examiners who were undercover. We wished to maintain control over lists of CIA examiner identities.

Heads butted and forehead veins bulged during several meetings, but management from both programs met once again to discuss a solution proposed by the CIA. Wanting to conceal the identity of the examiner who conducted each case, we suggested leaving that particular field of information blank. They complained, asserting that the examiner's identity was a required piece of information and that their computer program would not permit additional data entry beyond that point without it. Since an examiner's name was such a crucial bit of data, I suggested that my identity, as chief of the industrial polygraph program, could be inserted for every examination conducted by CIA examiners. The other agency wasn't very pleased with the compromise, but accepted it since it allowed for our immediate participation in their new record keeping system. As a result, dozens of polygraph examinations conducted every morning and every afternoon by examiners in cities across the United States for a ten-year period were recorded as being conducted by Alan B. Trabue. The other agency's records would prove my claim that I have conducted more examinations than any CIA examiner in history. Of course, the claim would be false since the records are inaccurate. Fortunately, the CIA's records do accurately identify the examiners who conducted every one of those cases.

Finally, there is the struggle to ensure that one's life-work continues. For much of my career, I strived to develop young trainees into competent polygraph examiners and interrogators. Young polygraph examiners new to the profession frequently treated the process as just another job, a new assignment with a new set of skills to learn and apply. With little life experience and even less experience as an examiner and interrogator, they often seemed to have little appreciation for the real gravity of their mission. I always struggled with ways to instill an awareness that their polygraph decisions could severely impact people's lives. I strived to ready examiners for cases that had far-reaching impact, for example, murder, terrorist bombings, secret nuclear programs, and weapons of mass destruction. The impact of an examiner's call can be far-reaching and affect innumerable lives.

The formal training for students in the Psychophysio-logical Detection of Deception Program (a basic polygraph examiner training course) contained a significant amount of time spent in practicing various polygraph techniques and interrogation. Life-like practice examinations proved to be significant eye-openers for students and were a tremendous aid to me as their instructor. The test subjects would participate in very realistic mock crimes, fostering a sense of guilt. Students would then practice polygraph test techniques used in criminal examinations. My role as an adjunct instructor was monitoring CIA students during their conduct of examinations, providing advice and guidance, and grading their performance. These examinations were very realistic and greatly assisted my efforts to instill a real sense of responsibility in the new examiners.

Struggle does not always have to be unpleasant. In the guise of good-natured competition, it can be a lot of fun. Several years ago, the new Chief of Instruction Branch noted that while there was a natural camaraderie between students from all the federal agencies, there was also a highly charged, competitive atmosphere in the school. Students were proud of the agencies they represented. They also developed huge egos as their skills as polygraph examiners and interrogators grew during the course. He decided it would be fun for the students' last practice test of the course to be conducted as a contest rather than just another routine practice examination. To prepare for this last examination, test subjects role-played kidnapping a baby, planting a bomb, taking a money box, or stealing a classified laptop computer. All the test subjects participated in the crime. All were involved with hiding the kidnapped baby, bomb, money box, or computer somewhere on school grounds. They were instructed to proclaim their innocence and deny any involvement in the crime.

The students conducted examinations of the test subjects utilizing a polygraph test technique designed to locate the missing item. The missing item could be hidden anywhere on the school grounds. Students determined the location of the missing item through polygraph testing alone. Interrogation was forbidden. Locating the item by any means other than the analysis of polygraph charts would result in disqualification. The contest required three separate polygraph tests. Each test consisted of three separate charts. Any student who did not conduct the required nine charts would be disqualified. Since they were unaware of the location of the missing item, instructors could only provide normal advice and guidance. Only the Chief of Instruction Branch and two contest helpers knew where the item was hidden. All students were required to start their examinations at precisely the same time. No student was allowed to search for the missing item without first obtaining permission from their instructor and a contest administrator. Obviously, the first student to locate the missing item was the contest winner. The winner would be awarded a trophy presented by the school director in a ceremony with all students and instructors in attendance.

I met with the other CIA instructors to develop a strategy that would provide our students the best opportunity to win. Just prior to the contest, I met with our students.

"Let me tell you my thoughts about how best to approach this contest," I said. "We will be given the crime scenario just before we begin. The missing item will be divulged and the rules will be reviewed one more time. Obviously, the first one to find the missing item is the winner. This is not just another practice polygraph examination; it is also a race. Your opponents will be all your fellow students from the other agencies. Don't look to your instructors for any special help. We won't know the location of the missing item. We will be monitoring you, and we will be available for advice and guidance as usual.

"Speed, luck, and skill are the three ingredients needed to win this contest. If you fall short in any of these three areas, you probably will not win. Speed is essential. You are competing with dozens of other students, each trying to get to the item first. You must not waste a single word during your test. You must not waste a moment of time. You must keep your interview moving along as quickly as possible. If you can give an instruction in five words instead of twenty, do it. An economy of words is essential. Analyzing charts quickly is essential. Moving quickly from test to test is essential. As I said, speed is essential. Wasted seconds may make the difference between winning and losing.

"Luck is essential. You've all had polygraph test subjects who produced poor quality charts, charts that were difficult to analyze. The winner of the contest will probably be lucky enough to have a subject who produces good quality charts. You've all had subjects who reacted clearly and concisely to relevant test questions because they had a heightened fear of detection. The winner of the contest will probably be lucky enough to have a subject who produces strong, clear reactions when he is being deceptive.

"The third essential ingredient needed to win this contest is skill. This is a graded exercise, so I will be issuing grades for all categories of your performance just as grades were issued for all previous practice polygraph tests you conducted. You must conduct a technically proficient examination, but I advise you to do so in a speedy manner. Remember, this is a race. You should stay in your examination room until you have completed your polygraph interview and are ready to come out to search for the missing item in the location you believe it to be based on analysis of your charts. If you come out to confer with me or to seek help with chart interpretation, you may be wasting precious minutes that will enable your fellow students to reach the item first. Obviously, if you are in serious need of help or guidance, come out of your room to see me. I will be there to help, but your best chance of winning the contest is to conduct a speedy, technically proficient examination on your own."

My strategy proved to be incredibly successful. What a contest it turned out to be. It was great fun for all. The exercise brought out the competitive nature of the students, and it brought out the rivalry between the government agencies the students represented. Unfortunately, we got off to a rocky start with the first contest. A CIA student was the first to locate a very realistic fake bomb that had been planted in the main building, and he proudly hefted it over his head in triumph as he paraded up and down the hallways. Unfortunately, when the administrators checked his work before officially declaring him the winner, they discovered he had failed to conduct the required number of polygraph charts. His instructor had been busy monitoring another student and failed to note the error. The student was disqualified and victory was snatched out of his and the CIA's hands. Fortunately, another CIA student was the second to locate the bomb. So the contest ended with the CIA as the proud recipient of the first trophy. I believe we also won the next contest. The third contest involved a kidnapped baby (actually a doll). A CIA student was the first one at the scene where the baby had been buried in the dirt behind the main building. The student had on high heels and hesitated walking in the soft soil. Her hesitation allowed the second person on the scene, a student from another agency, to rush past her to dig the baby out of the soil. We lost the trophy to the other government agency that time. After hearing the account of this contest, female CIA students in future contests decided to wear shoes with flat heals. One even removed her shoes and raced down the hallways in bare feet in search of the missing item. Another one of our losses involved a CIA student arriving at the scene twelve seconds behind a student from another government agency. I'm sure the student mentally kicked himself for using twelve seconds of unnecessary words during his polygraph interview.

The final contest I was involved in was probably the most interesting one of all for me. Prior to the conduct of the contest, I had my usual session with the CIA students to provide them with the strategy I had developed for giving them the best chance to win the trophy. Despite my reminder that it would not be wise to share our strategy with their fellow examiners, one of my students decided to tell a friend in the class about our session. Unfortunately for us, the friend was from another government agency who felt disadvantaged because her instructor provided no such guidance. She decided to complain to school management. Unfortunately, school management was already suspicious of the CIA. After all, we had won five of the previous eight contests and they couldn't fathom how we accomplished that feat. So, just minutes before the exercise began, they ensured that no instructor would be monitoring and guiding students from his own agency. I was assigned to monitor two students from another agency. Despite this last minute change, a CIA student was the first to find the stolen computer and win the trophy.

During my last three years at the school, the contest was held nine times. The CIA won six of the nine contests. The CIA's success in these contests baffled both school management and the instructors from other agencies. The specific test technique used in the contests was one used in criminal testing, not intelligence screening testing. This test technique was not one typically used by CIA examiners. No one could figure out how we were so proficient in its use and so successful. We were outnumbered by dozens of other students representing the other government agencies. They should have won the trophy many more times than the CIA. Considering the odds my students were up against, the strategy proved to be extremely successful. There had always been an air of mystery enveloping the CIA students at the school, but the mystique of the CIA rose to new heights following our uncanny domination of the contest.

Chapter Six

Covert Operations and the Polygraph Process

Liars are the cause of all sins and crimes in the world.

—EPICTETUS

During my thirty-eight years in the CIA's polygraph program, I traveled extensively to Central America, South America, the Far East, Southeast Asia, and Europe as a polygraph examiner. In addition to serving overseas, I managed all of polygraph's programs, including operational, applicant, reinvestigation, industrial, quality assurance, and support. As an educator, I served as Director of the CIA Polygraph School for six years and as an adjunct instructor at their current polygraph school for eight years. As exciting and challenging as all those positions were, my favorite was managing the CIA's worldwide covert ops polygraph program for five years. Also, beyond a shadow of doubt, a three-year tour in the Far East as a regional covert ops polygraph examiner was an assignment I considered to be unrivaled by any other.

Without question, I have tales from all of my assignments in the Section, but I'm going to primarily recount stories from covert cases conducted in support of the NCS (National Clandestine Service). During trips to countries in Europe, Central America, South America, and the Far East, occasionally things went wrong, usually because common sense and basic security was thrown out the window by someone. Overseas covert operations cases are conducted in an environment where the unexpected is to be expected and where best laid plans can go wrong. There are always lessons to be learned.

A covert operations polygraph case is composed of four basic ingredients: case officers, polygraph examiners, agents, and testing locations. Case officers and spies are frequently confused in the media as being one and the same. A spy is a human asset or agent that is recruited by an intelligence officer of a foreign intelligence service. Spies are not intelligence officers. Case officers are intelligence officers. Spies are recruited by case officers to engage in espionage. Case officers are those individuals whose job it is to meet, assess, and develop a relationship with foreign nationals overseas with the ultimate goal in mind of having those individuals work secretly for the CIA in some fashion, typically to provide us with information we cannot obtain through open sources.

Case officers may spend anywhere from days to years in the development of a person to reach a point where he will agree to enter into a secret working relationship with us. The individual is thus recruited, formalizing the deal. The case officer provides any necessary training and then handles the agent. From that point on, he routinely meets with the agent in secret to receive information and to provide the agent with new tasking.

Polygraph examiners overseas are typically on loan from the Office of Security to the National Clandestine Service. Examiners travel all over the world to handle covert polygraph requirements. Although foreign governments are aware of their presence, they are not aware of the true purpose of an examiner's visit. An examiner is subject to arrest and prosecution under the laws of the foreign country he is visiting. After all, espionage is a crime involving the theft and unauthorized revelation of classified information about the plans and activities of a foreign government. The agent, case officer, and examiner are all subject to arrest if caught.

The third ingredient in this operational mix is the agent. There are many types of agents. To name a few, there are support assets, access agents, political party penetrations, government penetrations, terrorist group penetrations, and intelligence service penetrations. Some recruited agents are the result of unsolicited offers from individuals to provide us with their services and information. They are walk-ins or write-ins. Most agents are part-timers. Whatever they do for us doesn't take up a full workday, five days a week. Some have actually approached us and volunteered their services, while some have agreed to collaborate with us only after a very long cultivation by the case officer.

Some agents are truly interesting, dedicated, professional people. Some are the scum of the earth. Some are traitors, deliberately betraying their group, political party, government, or country. Money is often their motivation. Some agents take huge risks and it is hard to hold them back. Some are reluctant to do anything, except collect their paycheck.

When they actually enter into a formal relationship with us, some agents believe they work for the Americans, some believe they work for American government officials, some believe they work for American intelligence, and some know they really work for the CIA. Since the CIA doesn't always have the most positive image around the world, some agents would be horrified to learn they really work for the CIA. There are seventeen separate organizations that form the U.S. Intelligence Community. The CIA seems to take the brunt of the world's accusations of perceived American wrongdoing and has been blamed for everything from the assassination of President John F. Kennedy to the 9/11 terrorist attacks.

I once conducted (perhaps it would be better to say that I started to conduct) the polygraph examination of an agent in the Far East who had been working in a secret relationship with two or three different case officers over a six-year period. All of the paperwork in the agent's file indicated that he was at first only aware that he was reporting to an American government official but was gradually made witting that his contacts were CIA officers. One of the test questions I drafted for the exam was, "Have you told anyone about your secret relationship with the CIA?" The test question had been approved in advance by the case officer.

When I actually conducted the examination and reached the portion of the interview that called for the previewing of test questions with the agent, he asked me to repeat that particular question. I repeated the question. Then with an expression of great concern, he bluntly asked if it was indeed true that we worked for the CIA. Of course, I confirmed that it was true, probably expressing some bewilderment at the same time. The agent said that he had been suspicious for quite some time but had been afraid to ask, knowing what he must do if his suspicions were confirmed. He said he could no longer work with us now that he positively knew the case officer worked for the CIA. He announced he had to terminate his relationship with the CIA immediately. He stood up and stomped out of the apartment without looking back.

Needless to say, the office was extremely angry over the loss of a productive reporting source. However, when faced with the fact that I was only operating on information that I extracted from the files they provided me and that the case officer himself thought the agent knew he was CIA, the anger directed at me quickly subsided. Some hate the CIA for what they read in the press about supposed activities. Some worry the CIA cannot protect their identity and fear they may actually lose their lives if identified by turncoat American intelligence officers.

The final basic ingredient in the covert operations polygraph mix is the location used to conduct the examination. Testing done by federal polygraph examiners in the United States is typically done in a controlled environment, usually in rooms specifically designed and constructed for polygraph testing. Testing done while on TDY overseas in support of Agency operations is usually done in one of three locations: hotel rooms, private residences, or safe houses (offices, apartments, or houses used for the purpose of meeting with agents). These three locations are not constructed with polygraph interviews in mind, so examiners have to improvise to a degree in order to get the job done properly.

One of my least favorite things to discover upon arriving at a polygraph test site selected by a case officer is that he failed to consider basic requirements: furniture, security, privacy, electricity, a bathroom. All of these requirements are fairly simple, commonsense considerations. All CIA officers in the field have been polygraphed as part of the applicant and reinvestigation programs, so polygraph is a process they all have been through themselves, perhaps more than once. They should at least have a rudimentary understanding of the polygraph process if they have any recollection at all of their own tests. Most have also participated in field polygraph examinations of agents. If their own personal experience is not enough, there are guidebooks on the use of the polygraph in covert operations available to them in CIA offices around the world. These guidebooks are concise and informative little manuals on the conduct of examinations in the field. Other than some of the more technical information about the polygraph process itself, most of the information in the manual is nothing more than commonsense reminders. I have been amazed at times on the lack of thought that goes into selecting test sites.

I've occasionally encountered individuals who feel that polygraph examiners are overly concerned about security issues during the conduct of covert cases. I understand the basis for their reasoning. Should not the examiner be able to put himself in the capable hands of the case officer? After all, the case officer is a highly trained professional. He is trained to do his job safely and clandestinely. He possesses country knowledge that the examiner probably does not have. He lives in the country and speaks the language. He has specific knowledge of the police and intelligence service capabilities in the country. It sounds reasonable that the examiner merely has to put his safety in the hands of the case officer. Unfortunately, since it is better to step lightly into the unknown than to rush in and be carried out, that assumption is absolutely wrong. Case officers can begin to feel comfortable in their environment. After all, they are operating in their home territory, their backyard so to speak. They can develop a false sense of security. They can grow lax. Some are even careless and stupid, just like there are careless and stupid polygraphers, plumbers, auto mechanics, managers, secretaries, and so on. Of course, the difference is that if you put yourself in the hands of plumbers or auto mechanics that do not do their jobs properly, your problems may not be fixed, but you will not be arrested and jailed. I found it to be prudent to always double-check on the security of polygraph examination arrangements made by a case officer. I had to know something about his job to make sure he was doing it properly. My freedom and my life were at stake. There is wisdom in the old English proverb, "Hope for the best, but prepare for the worst."

The polygraph process has been utilized by the CIA for over sixty years. It was first used in the Agency's attempts to validate recruited foreign agents. After its utility was proven, it was applied to the clearance process for applicants for employment. The emphasis of the program has always been on elicitation and interrogation rather than on analysis of test results. Polygraph Section's reports go to the Office of Security's adjudicators in the case of employee, applicant, and contractor cases, and the National Clandestine Service in the case of covert operations cases. Both have always preferred to make decisions based on information that the subject divulged rather than on a technical call based on an analysis of the subject's physiological responses. Occasionally, subjects decide to freely provide us that information during a polygraph interview, but frequently they decide it's not in their best interest to do so, and it's only the skill and determination of the polygraph examiner that convinces a subject otherwise. Examiners with the strongest elicitation and interrogation skills are the ones who are the most successful in the polygraph program.

People may be born honest, but they seem to quickly get over it. Honesty, like beauty, is only skin deep. People learn very quickly that honesty is not always the best policy. People lie. Liars lie. Honest people lie. Lying is a matter of degree, and it's all a matter of the circumstances that led to the lie—the who, what, when, where, why, and how of lying. You can put a dress on a monkey, but it's still a monkey; you can dress up a lie, but it's still a lie. Obviously, interrogation would not be necessary at all if examinees didn't make conscious decisions to lie to polygraph test questions. In each and every case, test questions are previewed and discussed with the examinee prior to testing with the polygraph instrument. Questions are explained, words are defined, and modifications are made to account for any thoughts, concerns, or issues the examinee associates with any test question. Testing is never conducted until the examinee states he fully understands each question and is able to provide a confident and truthful answer to each question as it is finally worded.

Examinees still lie. After all, lies are useful. Lies are told because they can get people something that the truth will not. When examinees make conscious decisions to answer test questions untruthfully, they do so in order to avoid the consequences that will follow if their wrongdoing is made known. The examinee believes telling the truth will bring about immediate negative consequences, while telling a lie holds the promise of avoiding all the perceived consequences or penalties. Depending on the type of polygraph case and the issues covered during the case, consequences might mean anything from embarrassment and loss of respect to a loss of employment and the income that goes along with it. Consequences might even include loss of freedom or life if the misdeeds involve criminal offenses.

The Hollywood treatment of an interrogation situation has certainly colored the general public's perception of real-life interrogations as conducted by federal polygraph examiners. In Hollywood's depictions, subjects are typically restrained, brutalized, and bombarded with questions. There are many good books available on elicitation and interrogation techniques, so I will not attempt to provide great detail on the topics. However, since many of my personal stories deal with polygraph and interrogation situations, I will provide a very basic explanation of what interrogation is, at least as it was practiced by me. Over the years, I invested a great deal of time researching the literature on my own and evaluating various interrogation techniques using a lot of trial and error. Trial and error is an absolute necessity. One cannot become an effective interrogator by simply studying books. Trial and error, the application of theory to real-life situations, is the only way an interrogator can decide what techniques and approaches best fit his personality and result in some degree of success. After all, the cleanliness of theory is no match for the messiness of reality.

Interrogators are thieves. They steal from each other. Their skill is dependent upon not only what they were taught and what they have read, but also on what they have stolen from each other. A good interrogator will monitor the tests and interrogations of fellow officers and discuss cases in order to learn different techniques and approaches. Interrogations frequently involve a lot of experimentation in not only what is said, but how it is said. An interrogator's tone of voice or show of emotion can make a difference, and there are always different ways to present logical arguments to convince or persuade an examinee to reveal his concern.

The art of interrogation is a polygraph examiner's primary weapon against determined liars. A simple, working definition of interrogation is the structured questioning of an individual in an attempt to persuade the person to reveal information he has decided to conceal. An interrogator's objective is to overcome the examinee's belief that consequences of telling the truth are worse than the consequences of trying to conceal the truth. Although there are many styles or approaches to utilize in the conduct of interrogations, there are three common elemental tools: rationalization, minimization, and projection. An interrogator will offer many statements to the examinee that are designed to help the examinee rationalize his misdeeds. He will attempt to make it easier for the examinee to verbalize what he previously decided was too egregious to reveal. The examinee will be provided with statements intended to minimize the seriousness of what the examinee did, minimize the consequences that would result from its revelation, and make it easier to reveal the information. Finally, attempting to lessen the subject's sense of responsibility for his actions, the interrogator will project the blame onto someone or something else. When an examinee decides to lie and is then confronted with that lie, he is filled with a tremendous amount of inner turmoil, confusion, and tension. He experiences significant mental conflict and indecision regarding the appropriate next course of action. The interrogator's elemental tools of rationalization, minimization, and projection are intended to lessen the conflict raging within the examinee to make it easier for the truth to be revealed.

There are many interrogation techniques and approaches, but there are some basic components common to most. After a deceptive response has been clearly identified on the polygraph charts, an interrogator will confront the examinee with that fact. No single aspect of an interrogation has greater impact than this initial identification of the deception to the examinee. This is the "shock and awe" moment of the interrogation. After all, the examinee probably lied about his activity related to the issue for years. He probably lied to loved ones, friends, and/or employers, depending on the nature of the activity. The documents provided to the CIA regarding his background probably contained a lie by omission, and the examinee probably lied to individuals involved in the processing of his documents. The polygraph examiner was lied to during the pretest interview and then when the question covering the activity was previewed and discussed prior to the test. Finally, he lied to the examiner each time the question was asked during the test. No matter how much fear and anxiety accompanied the lies, the examinee probably held on to the hope that his lies would not be detected. That hope is shattered when an examiner advises an examinee that polygraph testing has clearly identified an untruthful response.

Realizing that the examinee feels it's in his best interest to conceal the information and that negative consequences will result from its revelation, the interrogator should do his best to convince the examinee just the opposite. To accomplish this, the interrogator may propose to the examinee believable rationales that will serve to psychologically justify whatever the examinee has done. Rather than react with negativity to any information the examinee provides, the interrogator may actually portray himself as an advocate for the examinee. He may utilize sympathy, understanding, compassion, and empathy in order to reduce the examinee's inhibitions about revealing the information. The questioning may focus on why the examinee did something rather than on what the examinee did. Minimizing the seriousness of the misdeed may make it easier for the examinee to reveal the information. The interrogator may be very direct with the examinee, confidently presenting his arguments in a calm, matter-of-fact manner. His persistence, patience, and professional comportment gain the examinee's trust and confidence. He may use rational arguments to demonstrate the realities of the examinee's situation if he continues to conceal the information. There are quite a few approaches and styles. I have seen them applied by other polygraph examiners, studied them in the literature, and utilized a number of them.

The accounts of covert polygraph examinations mentioned in this book refer to the interrogation of agents. While it is true that I managed to persuade agents to reveal information that certainly was not in their best interest, the method of persuasion never involved restraining, badgering, or shouting. No physical discomfort was ever used.

There were no harsh lights or threats of physical violence. The goal was to always snatch the information out of the examinee's back pocket without his knowledge through the use of persuasive and rational arguments with a little verbal trickery. The bottom line is that every interrogation conducted over my thirty-eight-year career as a polygraph examiner was a verbal, nonhostile process. Words are power. Words are a weapon for the man who wields them well. In my opinion, the art of interrogation as it is applied during the polygraph interview process is really the art of communication, the art of reasoning, the art of persuasion. Those labels provide a much more accurate and descriptive representation than the art of interrogation.

There is standardized test coverage for applicant, employee, and industrial program polygraph examinations conducted by federal polygraph examiners. Test coverage for covert operations cases is quite different. There is no standard coverage in a covert operations case. Case officers are typically concerned about similar issues when vetting their agents, so test questions frequently cover like topics. It is not dissimilar to the application of the polygraph process in private industry cases in the commercial world, at least as polygraph was administered prior to the Employee Polygraph Protection Act of 1988. After all, when put in the simplest terms, a case officer is merely hiring an individual to provide him with information in a very discreet manner.

In the world of covert operations polygraph tests, falsification of reports is one of the most difficult issues. It is an important issue because the foundation for the relation-ship with a covert agent is usually the information he is able to provide to his case officer. It's a difficult issue because of its complexity, as there are many types of false reporting. For example, there is fabrication, where the information is totally made up by the agent. There is embellishment, where the agent has taken a piece of good information but added to it. There is exaggeration, where the agent has taken a piece of good information but amplified its impor-tance or meaning by flavoring it. Also, there is mis-sourcing, where the agent may have actually obtained the informa-tion from a low-level official but reported it as having come from a high-level official in an attempt to magnify the sig-nificance of the information. An extreme example of mis-sourcing would be if an agent provided the CIA with information obtained about his country's activities and plans that he attributed to a high-level government offi-cial, when in fact, he actually got the information from a janitor. I would not want the President of the United States to make foreign policy based on that information. In addition, there is withholding, where the agent falsely claims he doesn't have access to information the case offi-cer wants. False reporting is difficult to handle because the process of reporting information lends itself so easily to modifications intended to influence the recipient.

As a CIA polygraph examiner, I had my fair share of admissions and confessions during the conduct of polygraph examinations. Obtaining significant information during examinations was almost a daily occurrence for most polygraph examiners in the Section. Only the truly extraordinary or shocking confessions were great topics for discussion. Confessions about illegal drug use, crimes, mishandling of classified information, or concealing foreign national contacts were more frequent and routine, and usually were not worthy of discussion. In the operational arena, examiners' reports routinely contained information about agents revealing their secret relationship with the CIA to unauthorized people, providing the case officer with false information, and reporting information to other intelligence services without the case officer's knowledge. The more memorable polygraph cases, the ones most worthy of bringing to the attention of fellow examiners, involved extracting confessions of working against the CIA on behalf of a foreign intelligence service. Unfortunately, those cases were few and far between. Most examiners spend entire careers in polygraph without obtaining confessions from an agent who had been working against the CIA. Many had cases with polygraph charts clearly indicating that an agent was a double agent, but few got the confession. It is extremely difficult to get such a confession when the agent has absolutely nothing to gain and everything to lose. His relationship with CIA would be terminated, he would lose his monthly paycheck, and he would be responsible for the failure of his county's operation against the CIA.

Extracting confessions from an agent working against the CIA on behalf of a foreign intelligence service may have been an infrequent occurrence, but confessions of wrongdoing were obtained on a daily basis in all polygraph programs. Confessions from agents resulted in their termination, and confessions from applicants and contractors led to the denial of a security clearance. Some cases with surprising confessions became indelibly etched in memory, like the case I conducted in the Far East in the late 1970s. I discovered the agent had great difficulty keeping his relationship with American intelligence a secret. My first session with the individual resulted in a lengthy interrogation. He provided information concerning 40 people he felt compelled to tell about his secret work for American intelligence. His list included relatives, neighbors, and business associates. It was an uncommonly lengthy list. Agents frequently admitted to telling a few relatives or a few friends, despite case officer instructions to keep the relationship secret, but telling 40 people was out of the ordinary. Even with his extensive list of unauthorized revelations, his test results indicated that he had not told me the full extent of his unsanctioned disclosures. I was surprised by the test results since I failed to understand his motivation for concealing additional names after already providing a lengthy list of 40. Although disturbed by his lack of security consciousness, the case officer desired to salvage the agent. He scolded him and reeducated him on the necessity for maintaining a degree of secrecy in their relationship. Since polygraph testing had ended with Deception Indicated results, and the case officer desired definitive closure on that issue, I was asked to continue with the examination on my next trip to the country.

During his second test about two months later, the

agent provided several new names during pretest discussion and an additional 50 names during a protracted posttest interrogation. Once again, final polygraph testing yielded Deception Indicated results. His list from the two sessions was now astoundingly lengthy, but the case officer was unwilling to part ways with the agent. Under the assumption that the agent probably couldn't have more friends, relatives, and business associates than the 100 he already confided in, the case officer found it hard to believe there could be anyone else remaining in the city for him to tell. They asked me to afford the agent a third polygraph session on my next trip to the country.

Two months later I returned to administer his third polygraph interview. The agent made no additional pretest admissions, but once again he consistently reacted to the key questions. I had to interrogate for hours. In a piecemeal fashion, he provided the identities of another 50 or so people he had confided in. The sessions became farcical for me. The agent seemed unconcerned about letting 150 people know he was a spy for the CIA, and the case officer continued to desperately want to continue the relationship with an agent who was a security incident waiting to happen. I hoped that he would finally grasp the true extent of the problem when I pointed out that his newest list included the taxi driver who brought him to the testing site. The agent was an individual who was totally incapable of keeping his relationship with us a secret.

The issue of making unauthorized disclosures regarding a secret working relationship with the CIA was one that frequently yielded reportable information. Keeping secrets is difficult for many people. Some talk about their secret role with the CIA to brag. They are proud of what they are doing. Some confide in relatives to help explain their nocturnal activities. In an act of self-protection, some confide in people they feel they can trust in case something goes wrong with the arrangement they have with the CIA.

Interrogations conducted on the standard questions of a typical case at Headquarters also resulted in significant information being obtained. The issue of deliberately falsifying or omitting information on personal history questionnaires was one that caused CIA applicants problems at times, but usually for relatively benign reasons—such as listing incorrect or forgotten former home addresses, not providing the true reason for dismissal from a previous employment, etc. The bigger, more important issues were the personal declaration issues of illegal drug use and commission of crimes, but those issues were also covered by specific questions on the polygraph test.

I once conducted an applicant test at Headquarters, lasting several hours, that led to consistent, significant reactions on the issue of falsification of a personal history questionnaire. It took all the persuasive techniques from my interrogation tool bag to convince the applicant to reveal his concern on the issue. Ultimately, I obtained admissions that took me by surprise. I fully expected to hear something on the order of a tale regarding a former employment, the omission of information regarding a relative in prison, or the falsification of school records. Instead, the applicant recounted an event that occurred during his time in military service. He had been involved in a car crash—a very serious car crash. He received severe head injuries, trauma to the brain, and as a result of a subsequent operation, he lived with a metal plate placed in his skull. Unfortunately, his surgery didn't leave him problem free. Following surgery and recuperation, he continued to have problems and suffered from periodic, debilitating seizures. The timing and duration of the seizures were unpredictable. They would occur unexpectedly and would totally incapacitate him for a period of fifteen to forty-five minutes. Realizing that his affliction could hurt his chances for certain types of employment in the future, he broke into the military hospital in the wee hours of the morning, located his medical records in a file room, and fled with them tucked safely under his jacket so that he could conceal his problem after he was discharged from military service. When he applied to the CIA, he didn't include any information about his accident, medical treatment, theft of his medical records, or current affliction in either his personal history or medical history questionnaires. What made the information particularly alarming to me was the fact he was being considered for a position at CIA as a courier of classified information on airplane flights around the world—a job that required constant vigilance over loads of highly sensitive and classified information. I doubt if the CIA found it prudent to hire a courier, responsible for the safe transport of classified information, who had the unfortunate propensity to suffer forty-five-minute seizures.

Confessions were extracted from recruited foreign agents on a variety of topics. There seemed to be no end to the type of transgression they were capable of committing. I tested and interrogated a principal agent in South America who was in charge of a group of six subagents. On a monthly basis, the case officer paid the principal agent and assigned him the responsibility of distributing salaries to the subagents since the case officer didn't have direct contact with them. The principal agent would provide the case officer with signed receipts from the subagents at their next meeting. Through lengthy interrogation, I discovered that the principal agent kept half of the subagents' salaries for himself and then falsified receipts for the case officer.

During another interrogation in South America, an agent reluctantly admitted to killing an inmate in the prison where he was once employed as a guard. Well, that isn't quite right. Actually, the agent said, "The prisoner died on me." As I unraveled his story, I discovered the agent repeatedly dunked the prisoner's head in a bucket of water as he was being hung upside down from the rafters of the prison. The prisoner drowned. Imagine that. The agent didn't kill the prisoner. The man had the gall to die on the agent.

Actually, understanding a little bit of Latin American culture and the Spanish language, I realized that his manner of expressing the incident was cultural in nature. In American culture, we have a tendency to take responsibility for our actions by saying something like, "I dropped the vase." In Latin American culture, they tend to place the blame on the object by saying something like, "The vase fell from my hands." The more socially acceptable implication is that it was the vase's fault. Therefore, the agent's statement, "The prisoner died on me" was his way of saying, "I killed the prisoner."

Another unexpected admission resulted from an interrogation of an agent in South America. During wartime, he interrogated five captured enemy soldiers. When he finished questioning them, he herded them into a bunker. Explosive charges were placed around the bunker. The charges were detonated, and the bunker was destroyed, taking the lives of the soldiers and making their deaths appear to have resulted from an act of war. He was one of the most cold-blooded, black-hearted individuals I ever met.

Spies, cheats, thieves, crooks, drug users, drug pushers, wife beaters, child molesters, street thugs, and white collar criminals. People do bad things. Any examiner who spends much time in the CIA's polygraph program will have his chance to deal with them all, numerous times, and in short order. All that it takes is a verbal, nonhostile process called the art of interrogation—the structured questioning of an individual in an attempt to persuade the person to reveal information he has decided to conceal.

Effectual instructors frequently relate real-life experiences to illustrate and reinforce lecture points. This practice is usually well received and has tremendous impact on their audience. There are many adventures from my overseas travels that exemplify what can go wrong when basic security fundamentals are not followed. During my official TDYs, I have visited most of the Central and South

American countries as well as most of the countries of the Far East, some as many as fifteen times. Some of my fellow examiners covered more of the world than I did during their careers, but I would be surprised if any of them enjoyed foreign travel more than I.

The illustrative stories that follow are true, and they almost all deal with something that went wrong during the conduct of operational cases overseas. I do not claim that their narration will serve as a foolproof guide for the safe conduct of covert polygraph cases. After all, Douglas Adams once said, "A common mistake that people make when trying to design something completely foolproof is to underestimate the ingenuity of complete fools."

Now that the basics of covert operations polygraph testing have been provided, I am going to tackle the issue of operational security the same way I would tackle the task of eating an elephant—one bite at a time, or more appropriately here, one story at a time. Some may accuse me of using this as an excuse to tell some old war stories, and I wouldn't argue too strongly with them. On the other hand, I'm an ardent believer that stories from the past can be excellent learning experiences. After all, the past is what actually happened, while history tends to be what we decide happened. All the stories from the past that follow are true. I always tell the truth, even if I have to make it up.

Chapter Seven

Thor at the Door

One may sometimes tell a lie, but the grimace
that accompanies it tells the truth.
—FRIEDRICH NIETZSCHE

W hen administering polygraph examinations
to penetrations of a foreign intelligence service, I
always took into account that the examinee has
the power and authority to make arrests and probably car-
ries a weapon. Some foreign intelligence services more
closely resemble our FBI than our CIA. From my viewpoint, an intelligence service penetration was one of the
most dangerous subjects of all, and I always took special
measures to effect a safe examination.

First, I tried to arrange for the examination to be conducted in another country, if possible. It is prudent to take

the agent out of his area of control to a location where he can no longer go armed and where he does not have the authority to make arrests. If such arrangements were not possible, I tried to have the agent taken to an area where he would not have the support of his agency. For example, the examination could be conducted in a remote, secondary city. Second, I tried to conduct the examination in disguise so the agent would not be able to identify me. Finally, I tried to make posttest decisions based solely on analysis of the polygraph charts and avoided any posttest interrogation. If testing yielded Deception Indicated results, it was probably wise to let the agent believe otherwise. An interrogation may anger the agent, and an angry intelligence service officer has the means to exact revenge. It was also prudent to handle all other routine examinations for the office prior to meeting with the intelligence service officer. There was always the possibility that my identity could be blown during the conduct of his examination, even if a disguise was used. Why take the chance that an effective surveillance team could follow me to all of the other agents during the conduct of subsequent exams for the office?

The office in a large Southeast Asian city once had six examinations on their schedule for me during one of my visits. On my arrival day at the office, a case officer called me over to a window that faced the main street in front of the office.

He said, "See those two tan vehicles at the corner?"

I looked out and saw them at the curb, one behind the other.

The case officer continued, "You've arrived at a very interesting time here. The local intelligence service is trying its hardest to identify all of the Agency personnel at the office. They're surveilling everybody, particularly anyone who leaves at odd hours. The case officers you'll work with are going to run you through some extra careful SDRs (Surveillance Detection Routes) when you do your cases."

I said, "Okay, no problem."

Deep down inside, I had a queasy feeling in my stomach. I didn't like all the extra attention I was going to get and wondered whether the cases on the schedule were worth the extra risk.

As it happened, the very first case on the schedule was a penetration of the local intelligence service. Good security protocol would have placed him last on the schedule, but he was only going to be available during the first day of my visit. There was no choice.

The agent had never been polygraphed before. He was recruited and handled by the Deputy Chief, and we were going to conduct the test in his residence. It was a familiar location for the agent since the Deputy's home had been used for previous meetings. The agent was not told in advance that a polygraph test was going to be administered at his next meeting.

Before I left Washington in 1976 for my three-year assignment to the Far East, I had been issued a disguise that consisted of a moustache, wig, and glasses. Unfortunately, the office failed to notify me in advance of my visit that I would need a disguise to conduct one of the cases, so I didn't send it through official channels. It was still stored at my office thousands of miles away. Nevertheless, I needed a disguise to conduct the examination of the local intelligence service penetration in order to protect my identity. I talked to the Deputy about my need, and he directed me to a storage room. There were about five disguise kits that had been left there on a shelf by former case officers or current case officers away on TDY. He told me I could mix and match to my heart's content. I tried on all five wigs and selected one that seemed to fit the best and look the most realistic. I selected a moustache and grabbed a tube of moustache glue. Finally, I picked out some horn-rimmed glasses. This slapdash disguise was uncomfortable and hot, just like all other disguises I had worn in the past. With the disguise pieces on, I looked like a bushy-headed, scruffy professor. Even the casual observer could easily tell it was a disguise. It may have been laughable, but it was all that I had. Disguises, at least with me, were always comical looking. Instead of feeling like I was part of a masterful CIA deception operation, I always felt like I was Inspector Clouseau in a Pink Panther movie.

After work, the Deputy and I left the office. He toted the polygraph instrument and placed it in the backseat of a small sports car with a convertible top, a car that stood out like a sore thumb on the streets of the city. It was probably the only one like it in the country. To tell you the truth, I would have preferred an air-conditioned sedan. It was a fun drive through the city and out into the suburbs, but the sun was beating down on my head. The heat was searing and unrelenting. The street odors were overpowering, and the smog from motorcycles and buses was at choking level.

I had a wonderful dinner with the case officer and his family. When the after-dinner pleasantries were over, I took the polygraph equipment to a backroom and prepared for the examination. About a half hour before the agent was scheduled to arrive, I took my newly formulated disguise kit into the bathroom to glue on my moustache, don my glasses, and fit and comb my wig. The wig, with its elastic rim, was uncomfortably tight.

The agent arrived on time, and I was introduced as a visiting security official from Washington. The case officer and I talked to him about the polygraph test being the next step in his relationship with American intelligence. He was told that successfully completing the test would bring him deeper into the inner circle of trust and that we were asking him to do something that we had all gone through. The agent readily agreed to take the test. He spoke English well enough to allow me to conduct the examination in English. After I politely asked the man to remove his weapon and place it in the care of the case officer, I escorted him to the backroom where the polygraph equipment was already set up.

The examination took several hours. I encountered two problems. The first was that I was extremely uncomfortable wearing the disguise. The wig was so tight on my head that my scalp throbbed after a while. I had to excuse myself about every half hour to go to the bathroom in order to relieve the pressure on my head for a few minutes. Also, the wig and moustache were hot. Beads of perspiration kept forming and dripping down my face. I was afraid the agent would realize I was wearing a stupid-looking, ill-fitting disguise.

The second problem was much more significant than the first. The agent produced massive reactions to relevant questions covering the security of the "secret" relationship he had with American intelligence. The evidence clearly indicated that he had either been directed against us or had reported his contacts with the case officer to his intelligence service. The reactions he produced were significant and consistent. I did not interrogate. In a conversational tone, I asked questions on the issues trying to elicit any thoughts or concerns the agent may have had. I did not reveal the fact that his test results were clearly deceptive, and I did not accuse or confront. My attempts to elicit meaningful information were unproductive, as I was unable to extract any reasonable explanations for his responses. After hours of questioning and testing, I left the agent for a short time to brief the case officer. Needless to say, he wasn't very happy with my news. He had invested a lot of time in the development and recruitment of the agent. Despite his hefty investment of time and effort, he decided to end the examination. That decision was certainly fine with me under the circumstances. I went back to the exam room and gave the agent a status report on his polygraph results. I told him the quality of his charts was excellent, thanks to his ability to follow my instructions during testing. I told

him there were some small responses during the test, but
that I felt our discussions on the issues gave me an idea
of what had been going on in his mind. I led him to believe I was confident in the test results and felt that we
did not need to do any more testing. I removed the sensors
from the agent and walked him back to the living room
where the case officer awaited. They talked for a short while
about the arrangements for their next meeting and then the
Deputy walked the agent outside to his car and saw him
depart.

I packed up the polygraph instrument and gave the
Deputy instructions for bringing it back to the office the
next morning. After the agent had been gone for about a
half hour, I took off the torturous disguise, allowing the
blood to flow once again to my scalp. Inspector Clouseau
loved to put on disguises. I did not.

After waiting another hour or so to make sure the agent
was long gone, the Deputy and I left his residence and
hopped into his sports car. It was well after midnight. He
backed out of his driveway and started driving down neighborhood streets at breakneck speed, making a number of
sharp turns.

"I think there are two cars and three motorcycles
on our tail!" the case officer shouted over the roar of the
engine.

He reached speeds of eighty miles per hour on the suburban streets and barely slowed to make wild, wheel-
screeching turns at intersections. Sitting in the passenger's

seat of his convertible, I felt my spine jolted by every rut and pothole. My ears were pummeled by rushing air that made it difficult to hear.

I tightened my seat belt and braced myself against the dashboard. A head-on crash seemed inevitable. I felt helpless. Thoughts raced through my mind. Questions came easily, but answers were elusive. Did the agent inform his employer, the local intelligence service, of our meeting? Did he arrange to have us followed? Are they merely following us or are they going to arrest us?

The case officer continued evading our pursuers, making perilous hair-raising turns and sharp switchbacks.

After twenty minutes of reckless driving, he shouted, "There's still one car and one motorcycle behind us."

I was surprisingly calm and clearheaded under the circumstances. After a half hour of zigzagging through the streets, the case officer said he thought he had finally eluded our pesky pursuers.

"I'm going to make the next right turn!" he yelled. "Get out of the car and make your way back to your hotel."

He took the turn at the next intersection too fast and almost lost control of the car as it fishtailed through the turn. As the car slowed, he screamed for me to get out. But he didn't stop. The car was still moving!

He screamed, "Out, out, out! Now, now, now!"

Leaping from the car and racing like an Olympic track and field runner, I managed to prevent tumbling down the street head over heels. I tried to walk in a nonchalant manner down the street for a block or two and then turned down a side street. After walking for several more blocks, I was finally convinced that no one was tailing me. I stopped and gave my heart a chance to return to something that resembled a normal beat. I looked all around and saw no evidence of being followed or watched. I took stock of my situation and parsed out the events of the evening. Relieved that I was no longer being followed by the local intelligence service, I realized I now faced a formidable, new problem. I was lost! There was no traffic at all on the street. Not a single vehicle drove by. It was well after midnight and the city was miles away, but I had no idea in which direction.

You're okay, Alan. Keep your cool. You'll be okay. Catch your breath, get your bearings, keep a low profile, and make your way back to your hotel, I thought. *No choice but to pick a direction and keep on walking until you find a taxi. The walk will give you some time to take stock of your situation. Keep alert. You're in a terrible neighborhood right now, you're lost, you have no weapons, you haven't practiced karate for years, and the local intelligence service is after you tonight.*

I ruminated on my predicament as I walked. I was in the city, somewhere far outside the city, to be more precise. It was about one o'clock in the morning. It was stinking hot, oppressively humid, and I was drenched with sweat. Earlier that night, I had conducted a polygraph examination of a penetration of the local intelligence service. The test results were terrible. They clearly showed the agent had reported his contacts with us to his service. He was a bad recruitment who probably was working against us from the beginning, and now I was abandoned in the slums. For a twenty-nine-year-old polygraph examiner who enjoyed being on the periphery of covert operations, but had no desire to be beaten, tortured, shot, or imprisoned, it was not exactly a fun evening. I kept on walking; I hoped in the right direction.

I stopped periodically to wipe the perspiration from my forehead. At one o'clock in the morning, it was probably a very humid 100 degrees. Where was my hotel? I kept on walking, trying to find a major road and a taxi. I walked for miles. Luckily, I didn't see a living soul until I reached an area that was closer to the city. I smelled wood fires for cooking. I heard chickens squawking and pigs snorting. The dwellings, from what I could see in the dark, were crude and run down—shacks mostly. The neighborhood I had wandered into was not a place I wanted to be by myself early in the morning. I finally came across a road that had a little traffic on it. I was able to flag down a taxi that eventually drove by. Finally! I started to relax a little on the ride to my hotel.

What a relief! I looked forward to the comfort and relative safety of my air-conditioned room. Working in disguise, racing through the city, running from cars and motorcycles, and walking endlessly in search of a taxi—I was drenched! I had had enough excitement for one evening. Finally on my way to the safety and comfort of my hotel room, I kept reliving the night's events. Had the case officer been right about being followed or was he just overreacting? Was he paranoid? What if he was right? Should I continue testing the office's other agents or should I leave the country? My mind struggled with many unanswered questions.

When I was at last safely in my hotel room, I peeled off my damp clothes and took a shower. Far too excited to sleep, I stood under the flowing stream of water, closed my eyes, and tried to force myself to relax. My mind finally moved to more pleasant thoughts, and I actually started to think about how I was looking forward to the next city on my itinerary. It was a bustling, congested Southeast Asian city filed with exotic sights, sounds, and food. It was undoubtedly a hotspot for political intrigue in that area of the world, yet it was a veritable paradise for a traveling polygraph examiner. I leaned forward a bit and felt the cool water rushing over my head. While in that position, I heard someone begin to pound so hard on my hotel door it sounded like the hinges were going to break off under the assault.

BANG! BANG! BANG!

The local service followed me! I thought.

Then I realized they probably didn't need to follow me. They probably knew where I was staying from the moment I arrived in the country. Adrenaline hit me like an unstoppable freight train.

I felt absolutely powerless and vulnerable, like a prisoner of war stripped for a hostile interrogation. There is absolutely no worse feeling, and certainly no more defenseless feeling, than being confronted when you are completely naked. Visions of being dragged naked through the hotel lobby and carted off to jail were interrupted by a second round of heavy pounding on my door.

BANG! BANG! BANG!

Finally able to move, I turned off the shower and reached for a towel. I wanted to cover my midsection before they broke down the door and grabbed me. As I raced to the bedroom for my pants, there was another round of intense pounding on my door.

BANG! BANG! BANG!

The hinges creaked and the walls shook. My heart started to beat with great force, as if it was going to burst from my chest. The adrenaline kept pumping. I was certain the third round of pounding would break down the door. Convinced that the local intelligence service was trying to break in to drag me off to jail, I decided that the last thing in the world I should do was open the door for them. They would have to break it down to get me. I was not going to resist, but I was not going to make it easy for them. After slipping my pants on, I sat down on the bed and waited for the entry team to succeed in their assault on my door. I waited a long time, but the banging on my door did not resume. I thought the intruders had gone down to the front desk to get a passkey from the manager or out to their vehicle to get a battering ram. I sat on the edge of my bed for a very long time waiting for the next round of banging, but it never came.

At three o'clock in the morning, the mysterious, unexplained incident seemed to be over, but I was much too worried to sleep. If I slept at all that night, it was just minutes at a time. I kept reliving the agent's bad polygraph examination, the high-speed car chase through narrow streets, jumping from the case officer's moving car onto a lonely street far from the city, avoiding capture and arrest by the local intelligence service, and the frightening assault on my hotel room door.

In the morning, I worried what additional surprises the new day would bring, but I made my way to the office without any problem. As I left the hotel, my eyes darted suspiciously in every direction as I walked through the hotel lobby on my way out to the street. Everything seemed perfectly normal as far as I could tell. I saw no knuckle-dragging security officers lurking in the wings.

Arriving at the office, I told the Deputy all that had transpired since he dumped me in the street many miles away from the city. Both of us then went into the chief's office to brief him on the late-night door-banging incident at my hotel room. After listening to my story, he opined that it was nothing more than a drunk, wayward prostitute. I thought his theory was implausible. Nevertheless, enough had gone on the night before that he advised me to leave the country as soon as possible. I'm sure he didn't want to take the chance that the local intelligence service was aware of my identity and activities in the country and that I might inadvertently lead them to his other agents. I didn't argue. After all, the next stop on my itinerary happened to be one of my favorite cities. It held the promise of being a much more pleasant experience.

Chapter Eight

Poorly Chosen Test Sites

Half a truth is often a great lie.
— BENJAMIN FRANKLIN

A room constructed specifically for the purpose of conducting polygraph examinations typically contains a desk and two chairs for the examiner, one placed in front of the examinee for pretest discussion and one behind the desk to sit in while operating the polygraph instrument. The examinee has a chair with adjustable arms and a straight back. The room is sterile in appearance to prevent distractions during testing. There may also be audio and video recording equipment, and sometimes a two-way mirror to allow for observation by others. The walls of the room are filled with soundproofing material to minimize outside noise so that the examinee is not startled or distracted.

However, when I conducted examinations overseas in support of NCS operations, I had to improvise to create the best environment possible for testing in a hotel room, safe house, or personal residence. These sites are usually quite suitable, but sometimes locations chosen by case officers for polygraph interviews can introduce a challenge.

Once, in yet another South American city, I conducted a covert operations polygraph examination in a safe house. The case officer, George, escorted me to the site, located in a nice-looking apartment building. We rode the elevator to one of the upper floors, walked down a long hallway, and stopped at the apartment's front door.

"Here we go. This is it," George said.

He unlocked the door, swung it wide open, and invited me to enter first. Upon entering the apartment, I only needed to take a quick look around in order tell him that the accommodations appeared to be excellent.

"Nice. Very nice," I said. "While you are gone, I'll just skulk around the place to figure out where the best testing location will be."

"I thought it would be okay," George replied. "I'll leave you here and be back soon with our friend."

He left to pick up the agent from some street corner in the city to bring him back to the apartment. While George was away, I looked around the apartment. The furniture was a little sparse, but I knew that I could work with the chairs and tables that were there. The apartment was comprised of your typical living room, kitchen, dining room, and bedroom. The dining room chairs had hard, uncomfortable backs. I decided they wouldn't be comfortable enough for use during a long interview. The bedroom had no table or chairs. I decided the living room would be the most suitable place in the apartment to use. There was an easy chair that the examinee could sit in. I thought I would sit on the couch and use the coffee table between us as a place to set the polygraph equipment.

When George returned with the agent, I greeted them both and was introduced as Mr. Green, a polygraph examiner from Headquarters in Washington DC.

"It's going to take me several minutes to set up the equipment in the living room before we get started," I said. "I'll be right with you."

I busied myself with the polygraph instrument, but within several minutes I stopped to listen to footsteps coming down the apartment building hallway. The door to the apartment was about ten feet away from where I sat, but the footsteps outside got louder and louder as they neared. The owners of the footsteps started to talk as they got closer to our apartment. I certainly didn't understand every word. After all, they were speaking a foreign language. However, I could clearly hear every word. I looked down and saw that there was a two-inch gap at the bottom of the front door. I also noticed that the floor in the apartment was a hardwood floor. Focusing for the first time on the floors, I glanced around the apartment and saw that every floor in the entire apartment was covered with hardwood flooring—and not a throw rug in sight. Rather than being sound-proofed, the apartment's hardwood flooring had just the opposite effect. Noise was bouncing off the floor like a sounding board.

"George, we've got a problem," I said. "We can't very well talk to your man about his secret relationship with the CIA if anyone passing by in the hallway can clearly over-hear us. We'll bring a lot of unwanted attention on our activities in here."

Thankfully, George agreed with my assessment. I was hoping I wouldn't have an argument over basic security issues.

George and I tried stuffing the gap at the bottom of the door with bathroom towels. We tested this setup but found it didn't help. George stood outside in the hallway while I stayed inside, but unfortunately, he could still clearly hear me in the apartment when I talked. I tried setting up the polygraph equipment in the back bedroom, but George could still hear me when he stood outside in the hall.

I finally came up with a workable, albeit not very at-tractive solution. I set up the polygraph equipment in a small bathroom located in the back bedroom. I also stuffed tow-els in the gap at the bottom of the bathroom door. I bal-anced the instrument on top of the sink and turned over a trash can to use as my seat in front of the instrument.

"George, I'd like you to stand in the shower to serve as the interpreter," I requested, hoping that George would see the humor in the situation. After all, neither of us was accustomed to conducting professional interviews in a bathroom.

"If I must," he answered.

I was pleased to notice a twinkle in George's eye as he stepped into the shower.

"And, sir, would you please sit on the toilet with your back against the tank?" I asked the agent.

He responded, "How charming."

Thankfully, the agent was willing to do whatever the crazy Americans wanted. A steady salary can be a powerful motivator.

I wish I had a photograph of the three of us in that small bathroom trying to conduct a professional interview. I guarantee you that photograph would be nicely framed and sitting on my fireplace mantel at home right now to serve as a piece of memorabilia guaranteed to spark a conversation.

Unfortunately, the test didn't go well for the examinee. I had to conduct an interrogation in that bathroom setting, and it proved to be rather lengthy and uncomfortable for all of us. After all, shower standing, toilet sitting, and trash can squatting are not meant to be marathon events. The setting may have been comical, but the nature of our business was very serious. I hoped that the agent understood the seriousness of the situation, despite the fact that he was crammed into a small bathroom with two other men— probably not a typical daily occurrence for him.

In an attempt to reinforce the gravity of the situation, at an opportune time during the interrogation I said, "Do you know where your relationship with the CIA is going?"

The agent responded, "Huh? What do you mean?"

Then I thrust my arm toward his right shoulder, grabbed the handle on the tank, and flushed the toilet. I did this on the spur of the moment, purely for the dramatic and symbolic effect. I hoped that hearing his secret relationship and steady paycheck go symbolically swirling, churning, gurgling, and glugging down the drain might have impact. It didn't, as I recall, but it was worth a try. As it turned out, that was the only opportunity I ever had to use a flushing toilet as an interrogation tactic, and I am happy to say I never again conducted a polygraph examination in a bathroom.

The bathroom I used for a test site may have been uncomfortable, but at least it was located in an air-conditioned apartment. A testing site that is hot can certainly lead to some discomfort, but whenever I added a disguise into the mix, it could be miserable. The disguise I had been issued back in 1975 has remained unused in its case since it was issued. Every single time I had a requirement to use a disguise in order to accomplish the safe conduct of a covert operations case, it was always uselessly stored in my office thousands of miles away.

During one of my TDYs to the capital city of a Southeast Asian country, I discovered that one of the polygraph cases on the schedule was a penetration of the local intelligence service. He was a relatively new recruitment who had not been previously polygraphed. Since penetrations of the local intelligence service should be conducted with extra care by employing additional security measures, I made sure I discussed the meeting arrangements with the handling case officer well in advance. I quickly discovered that the case officer was as concerned as I was about conducting the case in a safe and secure manner.

"Alan, I tried to convince the chief that we should conduct this case in another country," he advised. "I explained that the agent is constantly armed and that he has a support team that travels with him every day. They are also armed. I further explained that we need to get the agent away from his support team to make sure that you and I are safe during the test. I added that the agent appears to be a solid recruitment and that I believe he has not revealed his secret relationship with us to anyone, but that we will not actually be sure of that until he passes the polygraph. Alan, I stressed that we need to conduct the case in another country for safety reasons. I suggested Bali, Hawaii, or the Seychelles. He kicked me out of his office!"

I knew that he was joking so I answered, "You failed in your mission. Ten lashes with a wet noodle for you!"

"Seriously," he replied. "We are going to do this right. You and I will be taking a car trip Friday afternoon far away from the city to a beautiful resort up in the mountains. I've got a room booked there already. The agent believes he and I are going there to relax and enjoy ourselves. His team will not travel up there with him. Once we meet there, I'll set his weapon aside and then trot you out to be introduced."

I told him the meeting arrangements sounded fine, although I would have preferred a trip to Bali or Hawaii.

As a final thought, I added, "Just one more thing. A disguise. I'd like to wear a disguise in case the results of the test are Deception Indicated. I wouldn't want your man to prevent me from leaving the country. Only thing is, I don't have my disguise with me."

"That shouldn't be a problem," the case officer replied. "I think we have disguises in the storeroom. You can use what you want."

Later that day, I selected bits and pieces from several disguise kits with a strong feeling of déjà vu. I tried on wigs, moustaches, and glasses. I finally found a combination of items that seemed to fit. With my new disguise on, I looked neither suave, debonair, nor distinguished. Despite my best efforts, I looked ridiculous. I thought it would be blatantly obvious to everyone that I was wearing a disguise. The best I hoped for was that the disguise would hide my features well enough to prevent identification. Also, to help in that regard, I planned on wearing shoes, slacks, and a shirt that I would not wear again during my stay in the country.

On the evening of the examination, the case officer and I headed for the mountain resort in his automobile. There was nothing remarkable about the drive through the city. The city, like most cities, was loud, dirty, and congested. On the other hand, once we were out of the city, the scenery was gorgeous. Mountains, farms, rice paddies, and carts pulled by water buffalo were much more interesting sites. That evening I saw a part of the country I had never seen before even though I had TDYed to the country numerous times. Outings like that one could make an entire

TDY away from home worthwhile. The country was wild, primitive, lush, and beautiful.

As we traveled higher into the mountains and neared the resort area, the case officer pulled off the main road to put different license plates on his car before we pulled into the resort. He turned down a side road that appeared to head into a farmer's fields. After proceeding about a hundred yards, the terrain around us turned rather hilly. He stopped the car, and we both exited. I watched as he started to switch the license plates on the car with ones he had in the trunk. As the case officer was busy with his task, I glanced up and noticed two farmers standing on the top of a hill about forty feet away. They stood still, holding staffs or some type of farm implements, and stared down at us. I informed the case officer that we had an audience. He stopped his fiddling with the plates, and the two of us just stood there and stared back at the two farmers—the scene must have had the appearance of a Mexican standoff. The two farmers eventually disappeared from sight as they walked away from us back down the hill. After waiting awhile to make sure they were gone, the case officer finished switching the plates, and we made our way back out to the main road.

Not long after being observed during our performance of the clandestine license plate switch trick, we arrived at the resort and checked into the hotel. The grounds of the resort were beautiful. I noticed tennis courts, swimming pools, and a golf course as we drove in. It was somewhat depressing to realize we were not there to partake in any of the pleasures the resort had to offer.

As we checked out the accommodations, the case officer remarked how much cooler it was up in the mountains. I agreed with him, but thought, *Right! It's gone from 110 degrees to 90 degrees. No matter how you twist the words, it's still hot and humid.* Then I noticed the room was not air-conditioned and thought about the disguise I was going to have to wear for hours. Previous experience with wigs and mustaches had taught me that they could be uncomfortable and hot.

Thirty minutes before he was scheduled to arrive, I put on my disguise and then waited in a backroom for the agent to make an appearance. Before long I heard the agent rather raucously greet the case officer, and I tried to listen through the closed door as the case officer explained the real purpose of their meeting at the resort. After about ten minutes, the case officer entered the backroom where I was waiting and said the agent readily agreed to be polygraph tested and was anxious to meet me.

After all the introductions were made and enough small talk was engaged in to ease the tension, the agent and I retired to the backroom to conduct the polygraph interview. Polygraph testing was actually accomplished in a rather smooth, uneventful fashion. All indications were that the case officer had made a sound recruitment. There were no indications of deception to any of the relevant questions I posed during testing. The problem that night was not with the polygraph test. The problem was simply the length of time it took to administer the test.

It has been my experience that disguises are horribly uncomfortable contraptions. It is simply unnatural and uncomfortable to have a bushy moustache glued to your upper lip. Heavy horn-rimmed glasses resting on your nose for hours on end leave something to be desired, and worst of all, a wig is a contraption invented by the devil himself. A wig that fits tightly on your head makes your scalp throb with every beat of your heart. To top off this masochistic concoction, simply add a generous helping of heat.

Even though the polygraph interview was problem free, I was miserable after a while. I was hot and started to perspire. I was sure the sweat on my upper lip started to loosen the glue, and I feared that my moustache would fall off as I talked to the agent. I must have looked ridiculous as I constantly reached up to touch the glasses, moustache, and wig as I talked. I even excused myself several times during the interview to look in a bathroom mirror to make sure parts of the disguise were not drooping or dislodging. The heat of a hotel room without an air conditioner in the tropics and a disguise are not a good mix. Although it sounds exciting to hear about a polygrapher in a disguise having a clandestine meeting with a foreign intelligence officer in a mountain resort on a tropical island, never forget that there is always more to a story than meets the eye.

A bathroom may have been my oddest site for a polygraph test, and testing in a hot room while wearing a disguise may have been extremely uncomfortable, but there is another site that takes the prize for being the absolute worst site. I have conducted polygraph examinations under extreme conditions: the sweltering heat of a jungle, the dryness of a desert, the humidity of a swamp. However, high-altitude testing sites are some of the worst I've ever encountered. There are quite a few countries around the world with high-altitude cities. For example, there are some located in China, Mexico, Peru, Bolivia, Ecuador, and Colombia in the eight to fourteen thousand foot range. There are even high-altitude hotels near high-altitude cities. The Kulm Hotel Gornergrat in Switzerland is over ten thousand feet high, and the Yeti Mountain Home Kongde in Nepal is fourteen thousand feet high.

Once, on very short notice, I was asked to do a case in a city high in the mountains. When international travelers arrive at the city, almost everyone experiences altitude sickness, a potentially debilitating, life-threatening condition. Visitors are advised to take it easy and rest as much as possible for the first twenty-four hours to allow their bodies to acclimate to the high altitude's thin oxygen levels. If you follow the advice, you will probably suffer through one of the worst headaches of your life, but it will pass. If you don't take it easy at first, you risk becoming very, very sick. The only treatment is to descend to lower elevations or to breathe oxygen. Severe high-altitude sickness can cause swelling in the brain and fluid in the lungs. Both of these conditions can kill you if not treated properly.

There are many tales of polygraph examiners and other Headquarters TDYers who suffered in this city's high altitude. One polygraph examiner passed out at the dinner table his first night in the country. His face landed right in a bowl of soup. During one of my previous trips there, an interpreter traveled from Headquarters to assist me with a case. When he failed to show at the office the morning after his arrival in the country, the office started calling his hotel room. When several phone calls to his room that morning went unanswered, an officer was dispatched to his hotel to check on him. The interpreter was discovered sprawled unconscious on the bathroom floor. After he was revived with oxygen, he carried an oxygen bottle with him for the remainder of his stay.

I had traveled to this city several times before. For each of my previous trips, I tried to follow the recommended routine of resting as much as possible during the first day to become acclimated to the altitude. During each visit, I could feel my heart beat almost twice as fast as soon as the airplane's doors were opened for disembarking. By evening, a severe headache would start and progressively get worse through the night, when nausea and stomach cramps would be unwelcomed additions to the headache. I would get little sleep the first night, but relief would arrive in the morning and acclimation would finish by the end of my first full day in the city. I quit smoking about six months prior to one of my visits and therefore fully expected a much more pleasant experience. I surmised that my clear lungs would surely help the thin oxygen get into my bloodstream. For whatever reason, that turned out to be one of the worst experiences with altitude sickness I ever had to deal with in

the city. I experienced a full twelve hours of severe headache pain that was accompanied by stomach cramping and
nausea. Death seemed like it would be a pleasant alternative. I probably should have gone to the hotel's front desk
to get an oxygen tank that they issued to tourists in my condition, but I was too incapacitated to walk or make a phone
call. Oh, the joys of foreign travel.

The purpose of my short-notice trip was to administer
a polygraph examination to an agent who had reported some
extraordinary information that Headquarters thought
should be corroborated as soon as possible. He agreed to
take the polygraph examination, and speed was of the essence given that the agent was only going to be available
for a short period of time. Since it was imperative that I
travel to the country as quickly as possible, I was on my
way within twenty-four hours.

The flight was miserable. I boarded a puddle-jumper
that stopped in five countries en route. The frequent up and
down nature of this travel gave me a headache even before
the destination city's altitude had a chance to work its
charms on my head. After arriving, heart-pounding double-
time again, I took a taxi into town, checked into my hotel,
dumped my luggage in my room, and then walked to the
CIA office. I was ushered around from office to office for
introductions. I learned that the meeting with the agent
was arranged for that very evening. I had a lot to do to properly prepare for the examination. I asked to see the polygraph equipment that had been secured in a storeroom by
the last visiting polygraph examiner. I hoped there was a

sufficient amount of ink and polygraph chart paper and that the previous examiner removed the D cell batteries before he stored the instrument. There was nothing worse than finding an instrument with corroded or exploded batteries. I was relieved to find the instrument in excellent operating condition.

I conferred with the case officer. He told me I'd be conducting the case in a safe house in the city and that another officer would meet me at a certain street corner in the city at dusk. I reviewed the case file and planned the test with the case officer, and I also drafted out the test questions and had them translated into the agent's language.

For health reasons, I should have been back at my hotel room taking it easy my first day in the city. However, duty called and there I was, dashing here and there, checking this and that, arranging, planning, etc. I was busy, but as busy as I was up to that point, I had enough free time to realize that my head hurt. It was a constant, head-in-a-vice, eyes-about-to-pop-out pain. It was unrelenting, except when I moved around—and it was much, much worse when I moved around.

I left the office around dusk carrying the Stoelting three-channel instrument. Built into a briefcase, the Stoelting polygraph weighed about twenty-five pounds. To keep a low profile while walking in public with one of those instruments, an examiner had to walk standing up straight, pretending as if the briefcase did not weigh a ton. That was difficult to do when there were many city blocks to walk. There was a standing joke in Polygraph Section that

foreign intelligence services could easily identify CIA polygraph examiners because their right arm was longer than
their left arm. In addition, as a result of the Stoelting's community inkwell system, in those days we all had ink stains
on our neckties and fingers. It is a wonder examiners were
not arrested based solely on the physical evidence that was
clearly visible to any alert foreign intelligence officer.

I walked for many blocks through the streets of the city
to make sure I was not being surveilled. Walking with a
twenty-five-pound briefcase significantly exacerbated the
altitude sickness.

The officer met me at the street corner as planned and
drove me through the streets of the city to an apartment
complex. We made our way from his parked car, entered
the building, and went up to the apartment. The officer
opened the door, and we both stepped in.

"Wow! Yuck!" he exclaimed after taking only one step
through the doorway.

"Oh, wonderful!" I sarcastically replied as I followed
him in and glanced around.

The apartment was completely empty. Not a single piece
of furniture was in sight. There were no tables. There were
no chairs. There was no furniture at all. As if that was not
enough to dash my hopes of having a routine examination
on a night I was feeling ill, I then noticed that there was
dust everywhere. Actually, it was more than dust. It was a
mixture of dust, dirt, and soot. There was a quarter inch
or more of it covering everything. It looked as if nobody
had been in the apartment for an awfully long time.

"Why, oh, why was this place selected for the examination?" I asked in utter amazement.

"The office is in the process of terminating this safe house," he explained. "In the event the agent's exam ends up with a call of Deception Indicated, he won't be exposed to a new safe house that we'll have to close down. I haven't used this place before. I didn't know it was going to be this bad."

Well, I guess using a safe house that was about to be terminated was a good decision from their perspective, but it sure didn't make my job any easier.

I noticed that it was starting to get dark.

"Hey, turn on some lights. It's going to be dark soon," I said.

The officer flipped some switches on the wall. The switches clicked, but the overhead lights remained dark. We both quickly realized that since the safe house was being terminated, the office had requested the power company to turn off the electricity to the apartment.

"Great! No furniture. And now no lights. Look, my instrument operates on batteries, but it's going to be pitch black in about fifteen minutes, and in order to conduct the session, I need some light to see. It's simple. No lights, no test," I said. "Also, as long as I'm complaining, it's been a long day, I feel sick as a dog, and I'm hungry and thirsty."

The officer said he would go out and find some lanterns or flashlights on his way to meet with the agent.

With as much displeasure that I could muster in my tone of voice I said, "Please hurry."

I may have been abrupt, but I was not very happy with the accommodations, and I was progressively feeling worse and worse. I was nauseated, my stomach was cramping, and the pain in my head was piercing, agonizing, and almost unbearable. The officer departed on his journey in search of light and a foreign agent. Within minutes the apartment turned darker than the inside of a sack full of black cats. I sat down in the grimy dust on the floor in front of a window in order to see some light from other buildings and a few stars in the sky. My head pounded with every beat of my heart—and my heart raced at about 150 beats per minute due to the altitude. The lack of oxygen, coupled with the highly discouraged physical activity that day, brought on nausea and stomach cramps of a nature I had never experienced before. Since no one was around to hear me, I sat there and moaned and groaned out loud while I rocked back and forth on the dusty floor. The pain was excruciating. I was on the verge of vomiting with every gut-wrenching stomach cramp, but I wasn't able to vomit. I was sure my intestines would explode any second. I was miserable. I waited for two hours in the dark for the officer to return. Two hours of excruciating, mind-numbing pain seemed interminable. Dedication and a gung-ho attitude will surely be the death of me some day.

When the officer returned, he brought the agent with him. He also had a cardboard box that contained a bottle of carbonated water, a candy bar, some matches, and about six candles. There were no lanterns. There were no flashlights. The officer explained that candles were the best he could do at that time of night on such short notice. So, try-ing to make the best of an absolutely terrible situation, I ate some of the candy bar, drank some of the water, and then set up the polygraph instrument on the dusty, grimy floor with candles spaced about every eight inches around it in a semicircle. I sat down on the grimy floor in front of the instrument. I asked the agent to sit on the floor with his back up against the wall, and I requested the officer to sit beside me to serve as my interpreter.

Throughout the entire examination, I felt horribly ill and was unable to control the occasional moan and groan as my stomach cramped and large midsection muscles con-tracted. The altitude affected me that night like it had never done before. The vise-like grip on my temples made me think of medieval torture chambers. The officer watched me with obvious concern, but I continued on with the in-terview. I was not going to quit.

The six candles that I had placed around the polygraph instrument added to the eerie, surreal atmosphere of that dark and dirty safe house. The wax from those candles must have come straight from hell. The devilish, malevolent flames played with my senses. They created an otherworldly, dreamlike atmosphere that played havoc with my oxygen-starved eyes. The flickering flames kept casting our shad-ows on the walls in the most eerie fashion. Our shadows on the wall danced, merged, separated, and at times even seemed to be locked in mortal combat. I couldn't shake the feeling that I was conducting a séance as we huddled around the polygraph instrument in the dark with our only source of illumination being the candles from hell. I wondered whether our psychic willpower could have levitated the polygraph instrument if we had all joined hands and concentrated very hard. Perhaps we could have conversed with the souls of deceased liars trapped in the netherworld. If there ever was a night to do that, that was it.

Chapter Nine

Tales of the Unexpected

A lie told often enough becomes the truth.

—Vladimir Lenin

Although polygraph examination rooms should be distraction-free, comfortable environments for the examinee, overseas that often isn't the case. The examinee's mind should be free to focus on the questions being asked and his responses to those questions. The room should be neither too hot nor too cold. Distractions, outside concerns, and an uncomfortable climate can interfere with the process.

A tropical jungle is NOT a comfortable climate. I once traveled to one of the steamy Southeast Asian countries to conduct an examination of an agent who was a penetration of the host country's government. He was rather well known. Frequent media exposure made him easily recognizable by people on the street. For that very reason, the office was reluctant to meet with him anywhere in the city. If he were to be seen in public with Westerners, his career might be over, and his working relationship with us would surely be finished.

The case officer, Jim, and the agent met on a regular basis at a safe house far outside the city. Their next meeting was scheduled to coincide with my visit. The agent had previously agreed to undergo polygraph testing, but he didn't know an examination was scheduled to be conducted at his next meeting. For fear of being seen together, Jim and the agent did not travel together. They each made their own way to the meeting site as a routine precaution.

After dark on the evening of the examination, Jim drove me to the safe house. It was located many miles outside the city, deep in the heart of an ever-encroaching jungle. As we left the city and headed off the main roads onto narrow, unpaved roads through jungle, the foliage around us became much more primitive and dense. The air became stagnant and thick with the oppressive humidity. The smell of wet, rotting vegetation started to seep through the closed windows of the automobile as we headed deeper and deeper into the jungle.

We bounced along on rut-filled roads to the safe house—roads that threatened to be closed off by the fast-encroaching vegetation before we could make the return trip. I had a premonition that the polygraph case had the potential to be a memorable one. I could not shake the feeling. Whether it was premonition, sixth sense, or plain old gut feeling, I don't know, but I do know it was impossible to have anticipated the events that actually unfolded that evening.

When we finally arrived at the safe house, the agent bounded down the steps outside the main entrance to greet us. He and I were introduced, and Jim explained that I was there to administer the polygraph examination.

"No problem. No problem," the agent said, although his smile waned and his features took on the appearance of a very worried man. "Only, I hope the accommodations here will suit your needs."

As I started to inspect our meeting site, I noted that the safe house was little more than a large shack with a thatched roof held up by pillars. As I entered the shack, I observed sufficient furniture inside to arrange appropriately, so I didn't think that was the issue. The walls only reached halfway from the floor, leaving the upper half to be covered with wooden blinds that could be raised or lowered. There were no windows. The shack was not an enclosed structure. It was actually an open-air shack with no air conditioning, and there were no fans that I could see. Of course, it was hot and humid inside. After all, we were in a jungle. In a Southeast Asian jungle at night, one can expect a cool 105 degrees on the average. That night it felt like 120 degrees. The air was not moving at all.

The air may not have been moving, but something else in the safe house was. As I took a few steps into the main room of the shack, the agent pointed at a huge swarm of flying insects and said, "Look, many mosquitoes!"

He was apparently a master of understatement. The safe house was filled with mosquitoes! I'm sure that my use of the term, "filled with mosquitoes," doesn't conjure an appropriate mental picture of what I actually encountered. I don't mean a few pesky insects buzzing around. I don't mean dozens of mosquitoes. I don't even mean hundreds of mosquitoes. It was actually a science fiction movie type of mosquito problem. They were swarming by the thousands. Anybody in the safe house who sat still for a moment was instantly covered with angry, biting, blood-sucking mosquitoes. Looking at that swarm, we both shared the agent's concern about the suitability of the shack for conducting a polygraph interview. After some deliberation, we decided to try to proceed with the interview. We soon discovered that the trick to maintaining our sanity was to not sit still. We moved, we swatted, we waved, we smacked, and we danced. Constant movement was the only thing that saved us from the hoard of miniscule vampires.

There was never any serious thought of aborting the test. We were mission oriented, and the U.S. government spent a lot of money to get me in place to administer the polygraph examination. The agent, as well, seemed to be as dedicated as we were. Swarms of blood-sucking mosquitoes would have been an excellent, and entirely understandable, excuse for him to pass on the polygraph test that evening. However, the agent never entertained the idea of refusing the test. We pressed on with the polygraph interview, applying our strategy of constant movement during my entire pretest discussion with the agent. Then the time for actual collection of polygraph charts eventually approached, and I had no choice but to tell the agent that he would have to sit absolutely still during the test (each test lasts about three to four minutes). Between the swatting, smacking, and swinging of his arms, he looked at me with what I thought was a look of fear in his eyes. Maybe he was just resigned to his fate that evening. Maybe he was cursing the gods. Perhaps he was plotting his escape through the jungle, or thinking, *You stupid, crazy Americans!*

It turned out that the agent was either a great sport or a little crazy himself. He followed my directions to the letter, even though he was instantly covered with blood-sucking mosquitoes each time he sat still. I will never understand how he withstood the hundreds of bites he received. Perhaps he was accustomed to being bitten since he lived in a tropical location.

Ah! You may wonder what I did during testing. Well, I stood behind the polygraph instrument out of the agent's sight, and as quietly as possible flailed my arms, jerked, twitched, and swatted to keep those blood-sucking demons off me as best I could.

The agent may have been a great sport, but he certainly got the worst part of the deal that night. Even though he volunteered to proceed with the polygraph interview, it wasn't easy for me to subject a man of such great renown and high political stature in his country to such treatment. Fortunately, the agent sailed through polygraph testing with favorable results. No extended testing was necessary and no interrogation was needed.

I've conducted my fair share of field examinations under absolutely horrible conditions. I've had to deal with the unwanted company of all sorts of critters, extreme noise, extreme heat, and extreme cold, but this particular examination with its unwanted guests in the form of thousands of biting and sucking mosquitoes in the examination room was certainly one of my most bizarre field examinations.

Just about the last thing I want in a polygraph examination setting is some type of insect or animal that can interfere with the test. Unfortunately, it's a critter-filled world out there, and sites chosen for the conduct of polygraph examinations sometimes get invaded by critters we would rather not have around. It's usually considered to be more of a nuisance than a significant problem, unless you actually have to flee the premises. I've worked in safe houses that had roaches, ants, bees, mice, spiders, centipedes, and lizards.

I once conducted a case in a safe house in another tropical Southeast Asian country using a Stoelting three-channel Executive Model polygraph instrument that was built into a briefcase. It was considered to be state-of-the-art polygraph equipment at that time. You can occasionally find one of those antique instruments for sale today on eBay from someone who cleaned out their garage or basement. They are displayed also in museum cases in Polygraph Section at the CIA. The three-channel Stoelting was used for decades by CIA field examiners. It had one pneumograph module, one GSR module, and one cardio module. The three components recorded respiratory activity, sweat gland activity, and cardiovascular activity. The instrument was powered by batteries and had a community inkwell system that had three pens leaving ink tracings on chart paper that rolled out to one side.

The case I conducted in the safe house progressed smoothly, as most cases did. We used the living room area of the apartment as the test site. The agent sat in a comfortable chair in front of me and just to my right, and the polygraph instrument was placed on a tall table directly in front of me. As I usually did during the conduct of a covert operations case, I stood behind the instrument and had my question sheets and notes placed beside it for easy access. As the test progressed and the chart paper rolled out, I was required to mark the chart paper with each question onset, question end, agent's answer, and question number. I also had to mark the chart paper with any anomalies I noticed, such as outside noise, deep breaths, or movements made by the agent.

It was a particularly unexciting affair for me. I found myself going through the same motions, verbal spiels, and explanations I had gone through thousands of times before. The routine aspects of the case made it a tranquil process. Midway through one of the tests, at a time when I probably lulled myself half-asleep with the droning of my own voice in the somnolent atmosphere of that room, an eight-inch-long lizard fell from the ceiling. As if it wanted to pick the most disruptive spot, it landed right across all three pens of the polygraph instrument. Its landing made a *Pa-Rump* sound that mixed with the sound of the pens scratching across the paper, creating something akin to a very brief scratching of fingernails across a blackboard. The lizard looked up at me, flicked its tongue several times, and then quickly scurried off. It was not unlike the scene in the movie, *Alien*, when the alien burst out of a man's stomach, screeched at the startled group surrounding the man, and then dashed out of the room as the group stood momentarily paralyzed. The lizard's kamikaze attack on the pens from its original perch on the ceiling made an absolute mess of the polygraph chart. A portion of the chart now looked like a seismograph recording. The totally unexpected *Pa-Rump* sound startled me out of that serene place my mind had been visiting, and I froze for a moment. I don't think the agent was aware that anything was amiss. With great clarity of mind and a small amount of wit, I quickly reached down and marked the chart with the notation "LFOI" (Lizard Fell On Instrument).

There are standard chart markings for common occurrences during a polygraph test, for example, DB for deep breath. There are standard markings for cough, sneeze, move, outside noise, etc. For many years, I worked closely with personnel at an eminent polygraph school as an adjunct instructor. I facetiously made a case for the inclusion of LFOI on the list of standard chart markings. They were not very receptive, but then again, in all fairness, LFOI has only been used once in the history of polygraph, to the best of anyone's knowledge.

Mosquitoes and lizards are not the only kinds of distraction I have encountered. Distraction, in a variety of forms, can interfere with the polygraph process. When I conducted a polygraph case in Headquarters, I was most concerned about outside noise being heard inside the examination room. Although the rooms are soundproofed, the door is the weak spot that fails to block all sound. Too many times I've burst out of my room to chew out several loud-mouthed examiners who stopped outside my door to converse. When I conducted a case in the field, I was most concerned about inside conversations being heard outside the room. To help prevent my conversation with an agent being overheard, I used the concept of "white noise." White noise is simply sound, music, song, or conversation that is designed to mask your voice, making it more difficult to discern your conversation from other sound. Just think how difficult it can be to hear a specific conversation among the many conversations going on at a cocktail party or sports event. Similarly, think about how difficult it is to hear the other party during a phone conversation when others are talking near you.

In the field, I often had a radio or TV turned on in the area of the examination to help mask the conversation with the agent. I once conducted a covert case in a very nice hotel room in the Far East. The room was luxurious, a suite actually, and had all the furniture necessary to comfortably accommodate me, the agent, and the case officer, who was going to serve as my interpreter. I selected the living room as the most appropriate place to conduct the interview and moved the furniture around slightly so that tables and chairs were configured properly for the interview and testing. The hotel room had a TV located off to my side. I turned it on to provide the white noise I wanted to help mask our conversation. Shows with a lot of action, like bombings, shootings, fistfights, etc., would not be appropriate and might actually be distracting. I finally selected a channel that looked and sounded like it might be a daytime soap opera show with a great deal of talking. It seemed like the perfect selection, but, of course, I couldn't be certain because I didn't speak the language. The TV was not in the agent's line of sight, but the case officer and I were positioned so that we could see it out of the corner of our eyes.

The interview progressed smoothly and was well on its way to become one of many routine, unremarkable covert cases I conducted in an exotic Far East country. There is absolutely nothing wrong with a routine case, in fact, I prefer them and have been involved in scores of them. As my interview with the agent progressed, I clearly heard people on the TV show talking back and forth, and I was able to see a little bit of the show out of the corner of my eye from time to time. However, the TV show interrupted my pretest discussion with the agent as the characters' dialogue turned to moans and groans, unmistakably of an erotic, sexual nature. I glanced over and discovered that what I initially thought was a soap opera was actually a graphic, sexually explicit, hardcore, pornographic movie. The moans and groans also piqued the case officer's curiosity. His full attention wandered from his interpreter duties as he glanced over at the TV. The agent, who was facing away from the TV, tried to turn around to see the scene that was so obviously coming to a rousing and climactic end behind him.

I'm as patriotic, mission oriented, and hard working as the next guy, and I tried my hardest to not let the movie distract me, but I found myself glancing at the TV far too frequently. I may be a polygraph examiner, but I'm still human. At last, I changed the channel and continued with the interview without the distraction that I had inadvertently created. With everyone's full attention on the business at hand, the agent's polygraph test was successfully completed with No Deception Indicated results.

Chapter Ten

The Inebriated Case Officer

The truth is always the strongest argument.

—SOPHOCLES

The last stop at the end of my three-year tour in the Far East took me to one of the countries of the world I always wanted to visit. The offices in this country rarely requested the services of the regional polygraph office, so I felt extremely fortunate for the opportunity to finally pay a visit. There were three polygraph cases originally on the schedule; two in a secondary city and one in the capital city. The first two cases canceled, but not before I had actually arrived in the city. To my delight, I had a day to see a bit of the city before traveling to the capital.

The polygraph examination requested by the office in

the capital was quite an important one: a newly recruited, high-level East European diplomat. After getting settled in at the office, I went through the usual routine of reading the file, discussing the case and test coverage with the case officer, Martin, preparing the test questions, checking out the polygraph equipment, and reviewing the security of the meeting arrangements. I was pleased with the arrangements and expected to conduct a routine examination in a safe and secure manner.

Martin's plan was not complicated. He was going to drive by my hotel that evening in order to rendezvous with me at an intersection near the hotel entrance. I placed the polygraph instrument in his care, along with my notes and questions for the interview, and he planned to have it in his car when he met me near the hotel. Martin was going to drive me to his house and deposit me there to set up the polygraph equipment in one of his backrooms. He would then head off to scoop up the agent at another street corner in the city and escort him back to the residence. The agent had previously agreed to take a polygraph examination as part of the secret working relationship he had with the CIA. He knew he was going to take a polygraph test that evening, but he wasn't told where it would take place. I was to be introduced to the agent as Mr. Johnson, a throwaway alias I chose just for the conduct of the test.

That evening I arrived at the appointed intersection about ten minutes early and waited. Ten minutes went by, then a half hour. After more than an hour of standing at the intersection without any sign of the case officer, I was on the verge of returning to my hotel. I was bewildered and I was angry, but as I took the first step back toward my hotel, he drove up and stopped right where I was standing. As I climbed into the passenger's side of the front seat, I noticed someone sitting in the backseat. Martin introduced me to the agent.

The last thing in the world I wanted was for an East European diplomat spy knowing that I'm staying at the hotel at the intersection. If testing went south, he'd have no trouble at all discovering my true identity (best-case scenario) or exacting his revenge (worst-case scenario). I was not happy as Martin drove away from my hotel toward his house. I was worried. This type of total disregard for utilizing sound security procedures was not conducive to achieving my goal of staying out of prison and/or harm's way. Martin offered the explanation that he was running very late and decided to pick up the agent on the way to my hotel in order to save time. I am sure that from his perspective it seemed like the right thing to do at the time, but from my viewpoint Martin seemed to have tossed tradecraft out of the window for the sake of convenience. My safety was obviously at the bottom of the case officer's list of concerns.

During the ride to the case officer's residence, it quickly became apparent that he and the agent were two birds of a feather. They were both loud and boisterous—both back-slapping types. They had a grand old time, talking and laughing all the way on the ride through suburban neighborhoods to the case officer's house.

I thought, *Here I go again. More big mouths run by small minds.*

I tried to pay as little attention as possible to their conversation and concentrated on taking in the new sights during the drive. I think I shall never tire of looking out the windows of cars, buses, trains, and airplanes. Not only shall I never tire of it, I shall never stop looking forward to it.

After arriving at the case officer's home, he suggested that we all partake in a round of liquid refreshments in the form of some hard hooch before we got down to business. I told Martin I didn't want a drink and preferred that the agent didn't drink until after the test. He was clearly not happy with my response to his suggestion, and he pushed the issue several times, finally stopping when he realized I meant what I said. Obviously anxious to satisfy a powerful thirst, he started drinking by himself. Having won the short argument with Martin, I took the polygraph equipment to the backroom and made preparations to conduct the interview. When I returned to the living room, I noticed the case officer pouring for at least the second time, perhaps even the third or fourth, for all I knew.

I escorted the agent to the backroom to conduct the examination. The entire polygraph interview, including all of the discussions, explanations, reviews, and testing, was accomplished in about a two-hour period. No problems surfaced, and there were no indications of deception in the agent's responses to the test questions. I left the agent alone for a minute to bestow the good news to Martin who had been waiting alone in the living room during the two-hour session. As I approached Martin, it was painfully obvious he had continued to belt down more drinks while I had been working. His speech was slurred, and he appeared to be unsteady on his feet. He was thrilled with the results of the test on his new recruitment but made me repeat myself several times before the good news seemed to truly register. His thinking was obviously fogged by too much alcohol.

After I brought the agent back to the living room, Martin announced that we should all celebrate the successful completion of the polygraph examination with a drink. The agent accepted (no surprise there), but I declined.

I said, "Thanks, but no thanks. I have a bit of a travel headache. However, I'd love to have a soft drink if you have one."

They both laughed heartily at me and started belting down drinks. I watched them replenish their drinks and empty their glasses several times. Then they both started to persistently and forcefully goad me to join them. The cajoling became a game for them. Their attempts to pressure me were unrelenting, but I steadfastly declined. They thought my refusal to have a drink was funny, and they seemed to delight in their attempts to have me join them. As their attempts to pressure me continued, the agent tried to provoke me into drinking by trying a harder line of attack. He said something like, "What's the matter? Aren't you allowed to drink with a communist? Are you afraid you'll lose control? Are you afraid to bend the rules, or do you have to check with Headquarters first?"

They both laughed heartily, obviously thinking the

situation to be uproariously funny and admiring each other's wit. They both kept on drinking. When they had enough to drink (I thought they might need gills to continue breathing), the case officer suggested that we all go out to dinner together. His suggestion hit me like a wet sack of potatoes. It violated all the basic security guidelines I'd been taught. Was alcohol affecting his thinking that much or was operational security just not part of his thinking process? After all, we did start out the evening with him picking me up outside my hotel with the agent in the car. First, I did not feel it was prudent or appropriate to go out in public with the East European diplomat. It was a bad idea that put everyone's security in jeopardy. It was safe to assume that the local government suspected who I was when I entered the country, and I also thought it was safe to assume that Martin's affiliation with American intelligence was either known or suspected. Second, I did not particularly like these two men. I chose not to show disrespect for the case officer in front of his agent, so I didn't tell him about the operational security concerns I had. Instead, I expressed a desire to go back to my hotel to get some sleep. Displeased with my response, they both kept on pushing me to join them for dinner. I kept on refusing. Finally, when they tired of pushing me, they agreed to leave for dinner and drop me off at my hotel on the way.

After we all got in the case officer's car, the two of them in the front and me in the rear, we started our journey back to my hotel. Within the first two minutes of the trip, I realized I'd made a huge mistake. The case officer could barely keep the car on the road. He was snockered, and his attention was frequently diverted as the two of them laughed and joked their way through traffic. It would have been much safer if I had either walked or called a taxi, but once we were on our way it was hard to back out. It proved to be a scary ride, but at last I was safely returned to my hotel. After bidding them a good night and wishing them a safe journey, I stood on the sidewalk and watched the two of them drive off in the distance and reflected on what a different (and unpleasant) experience the evening had been. It certainly was not the evening I had expected or planned on.

Martin had agreed to bring the polygraph equipment (along with my charts, notes, and questions) into the office the next morning. We agreed to meet at ten o'clock. Sitting at the office the next morning, I watched as ten, eleven, and twelve o'clock came and went. He finally blessed the office with his appearance rather late in the afternoon and told me the story of what happened with the agent after I was delivered to my hotel. Like the *Gilligan's Island* "three-hour tour," their trip to dinner turned out to be a little longer than anyone expected. The two of them never had dinner. They made their way safely to a restaurant but just kept on drinking. On his way back home late at night, Martin was stopped by the police just several blocks from his house. He said he managed to talk his way out of a ticket. I'm surprised he was able to talk.

A few years later, I was informed that Martin was fired by the Agency. I assume his propensity to imbibe a bit too much finally caught up with him. When I learned of Martin's fate, I couldn't help remembering that night when an alcoholic case officer, a jovial, high-ranking foreign diplomat, and a no-nonsense, mission-oriented polygraph examiner made a bad mix.

The alias I used with the agent that day would not have protected my identity if he wanted to discover who I was. I was registered at the hotel under my true name. I always traveled in true name, but to protect my identity, I used an alias when introduced to agents. Like the great comedian W. C. Fields, I always wanted to use funny-sounding names like Filibuster Fogbottom, Theopolis Thistlethwait, or Throckmorton P. Gildersleeves. Unfortunately, I had been taught to use something simple and boring like Mr. Johnson, Mr. Brown, or Mr. Green. The alias I selected was recorded in my report of a polygraph examination so that I could use the same name if I ever retested the agent.

Foreign travel offered one other opportunity to have a bit of fun with words, but I was always too pragmatic to take advantage of the occasion. Another impediment was my observation that immigration officials around the world seemed to have no sense of humor. Whenever I completed immigration cards on the airplane just before landing in each country, I always wrote, "Official Business," when questioned about the purpose of my travel. I always felt a little uneasy providing such a terse answer. Writing the answer multiple times on every one of my trips made me want to write something silly like, "My purpose is to fight evil, no matter what form it takes, in a brave and noble quest for truth, justice, and the American way. After all, what is the measure of a warrior for truth? I think it is battling insurmountable odds to spit your last bloody breath in the face of the enemy and snatch victory from the jaws of defeat. I think it is being born with the bark on. I think it is facing the enemy without fear, giving no quarter, and taking no prisoners. The purpose of my visit is to vanquish America's enemies through the judicious application of trickery, cunning, and guile." Thankfully, I do have a little self-restraint. I am sure it was prudent of me to keep the urge to write such nonsense in check; I always had the good sense to write "Official Business" on the form.

I once traveled on a multi-country, six-week long TDY through South America with a female polygraph examiner. We accompanied each other during the conduct of most of the polygraph examinations, at first for her to watch and learn from me and then later for me to watch and critique her. At the beginning of the trip we arranged for ourselves to be introduced to the agents with names like Mr. Green and Ms. Brown, but purely for the fun of it, we decided to start introducing ourselves as Mr. and Mrs. Johnson. We explained to the examinees that we were a husband-and-wife team of polygraph examiners traveling together from Washington DC. We expected to get questions but I don't think we got a single comment. Toward the end of the TDY we changed our modus operandi, again just for the fun of it. We started to introduce ourselves as famous American couples to see if we could get more inquiries from the agents. We were introduced to agents as Ricky and Lucy, Fred and

Ethel, Mickey and Minnie, Sonny and Cher, etc. None of them ever raised an eyebrow.

Our little joke may have fallen on deaf ears and uncomprehending minds in South America, but it actually caused quite a stir back home in Washington. Our polygraph reports were being read by coworkers in our office at Headquarters. It didn't escape the readers of our reports that we started introducing ourselves as husband and wife after traveling together for a few weeks. We were the brunt of a lot of jokes and speculation about the onset of a real romantic relationship, and we got an earful when we eventually returned home. The ribbing and interrogations were unrelenting. As a result of our antics on the road, I'm of the opinion there are still people today who believe we had an affair during that TDY.

Chapter Eleven

Extreme Nervousness

A single lie destroys a whole reputation of integrity.

—Baltasar Gracian

C AUTION! DANGER! WARNING! During the conduct of field examinations, a polygraph examinee's extreme nervousness should be taken as a warning sign. Unfortunately, I believe most polygraphers have such a can-do attitude that warning signs are frequently ignored. I think our mission-oriented approach is our Achilles' heel and may be responsible for one of us landing in a foreign jail someday. Throughout my career in operational polygraph, I did what I could to make sure the next CIA officer in jail was not one of the examiners I trained.

Much of my career involved training activities in

Polygraph Section in one form or another. I was in charge of the CIA Polygraph School for about six years, and in later years I was involved in the training of new examiners, including working as adjunct instructor at another renowned polygraph training institution. In addition, I consider myself fortunate to have accompanied more than a dozen examiners on their first overseas TDYs to teach them the operational methods and administrative procedures of conducting covert cases in support of NCS operations. As my training trip instructor did with me, I always stressed the practice of applying sound safety and security measures to tests conducted in the field.

I once traveled with an examiner, Norma, on her very first overseas trip to conduct covert cases. Our first stop was a South American metropolis that is unquestionably one of my favorite cities. It is a beautiful city with a heavy European influence. Many visitors consider the restaurants to be unrivaled on the entire continent. Based on my own epicurean adventures throughout South America, I would not argue with them. When I reflect on all the countries of the world I have visited, I realize that some of my finest gastronomic experiences were in that city's restaurants. The city also has shops, cafés, and movie theaters galore, offering plenty to do and plenty to see for a visitor from Washington. It was a stop in paradise for visiting polygraph examiners. If one were so inclined, it was a stop where you could drink like an elephant, eat like a lion, and party like a monkey in heat.

The caseload of a typical trip is usually so heavy that an examiner barely has time to complete the work before moving on to the next country. Sightseeing and shopping were usually unattainable luxuries for visiting polygraph examiners. Norma's trip turned out to be a delightful surprise, since in this case the tests scheduled were few and far between. I had time to show Norma many of the historical areas of the city. We also had ample opportunity to sample the cuisine in some fabulous restaurants. Unfortunately, on our second day there, Norma contracted a walloping case of Montezuma's Revenge, also known as the Tijuana Two-Step, but more commonly referred to as traveler's diarrhea. She was miserable with this highly inconvenient affliction, but maintained a positive attitude and still managed to thoroughly enjoy the city with me. Night after night we dined on enormous amounts of some of the finest food in South America. Norma was bound and determined to not let stomach problems interfere with the pleasures of dining, day-long walking, sightseeing, or shopping tours of the city. Norma was tall, with legs that seemed to reach her shoulders, and I had to push myself to match her walking stride. She was the best walking partner I ever traveled with overseas. She enjoyed every minute of the outings. I simply had to find her a bathroom every once in a while.

The first case on our schedule required the use of the agent's case officer, Tom, as the interpreter. The agent had not been polygraphed before. He was a host government official, but not a member of any police, security, or intelligence service. From all information gleaned from both the agent's file and my conversations with Tom, I expected a routine, short polygraph examination. Norma was at my side at the office as I reviewed the file, prepared test questions, checked out the polygraph equipment, conferred with Tom, and checked on the security of the meeting arrangements. I wanted to make sure Norma learned all the steps to properly prepare for a covert operations case. I especially wanted to ensure that Norma watched as I confirmed with the case officer that appropriate tradecraft would be employed to provide for a safe and secure polygraph examination.

The case was conducted in a large suite in one of the city's grand old hotels, situated on the widest avenue of the city. The hotel lobby was lush, ornate, and alive with activity. People constantly hustled and bustled about. The hotel suite proved to be an excellent location for the conduct of a polygraph interview, as it was comfortable and very quiet. It had a large living room, a separate sitting room, a bedroom, and two bathrooms.

Tom took the two of us to the suite first. While I set up the polygraph equipment in the sitting room, Tom left us in order to meet with the agent elsewhere in the city and escort him back to the hotel suite. The agent knew he was going to have a polygraph examination administered by security officers visiting from Washington, but he was not told the location of the interview in advance.

When Tom returned with the examinee, it was abundantly clear that the agent was very, very nervous. My first impression was that he acted like Rodney Dangerfield. He couldn't stand still, his eyes darted from side to side, and he constantly picked at his clothes and tugged at his collar. He repeatedly sucked on a cigarette that was not lit.

"Do you have a match?" he asked me.

When he spoke he was wide-eyed and very animated. He shifted back and forth on his feet, and his eyes kept searching the room. His arms were in constant motion.

"Sorry, I don't smoke," I replied.

I was fascinated and a little mesmerized by his jittery motions, but his behavior started to worry me. I wondered whether he was normally that tense or on his thirty-seventh cup of coffee that day.

"Do you have a match?" he asked Norma in desperation.

He acted like a heroin-addicted man who was looking urgently for his next fix as debilitating withdrawal symptoms set in.

"No," she answered. "Sorry."

The case officer, who had been interpreting for us, said in English, "He's been jittery since I picked him up. He can't seem to stay still, and he's constantly asking for a stupid match."

The agent embarked on a frenzied inspection of the various rooms in the hotel suite in search of a match, but he discovered there were no matches anywhere in the suite. He started to head out the door, but I stopped him and asked where he was going. He told me he wanted to go down to the lobby to get a match. I motioned for him to wait for a minute. With some urgency I pulled Tom aside.

"Tom, is this guy's behavior right now in any way normal or typical?" I queried.

"I've never seen him this way," he answered.

"Well, we can't let him go to the lobby. We've got to keep him here in our sight at all times. This could be a ploy to get away from us to make a phone call," I spoke in a very somber tone with a hint of alarm in my voice to make sure he understood the seriousness of the situation. My suggestion was obviously a worst-case scenario, but I felt it was imperative that Tom realize the potential consequences. Fortunately, Tom agreed with me.

Although the agent seemed to be in constant movement, I made sure I had his attention and with a firm, authoritative tone I said, "Look, settle down. You are simply going to have to wait until after the interview to smoke a cigarette. My time is very valuable. I have other appointments this evening, and we can't waste any more of my time in search of matches so you can smoke. Calm down. Surely you can go without a cigarette for a little while?"

He stared at me while contemplating what I said, and he actually seemed to relax a little. I noticed a change in his nervous demeanor—he went from acting exactly like Rodney Dangerfield to someone doing a poor imitation of Rodney Dangerfield. At the time, I thought I was witnessing an extreme case of pretest jitters, but I knew that general nervousness typically lessened when examinee's learned something about the interview process.

"Please," I said. "I know that Tom has told you a little about the requirement for you to undergo a polygraph interview. All of us in this room have also gone through the polygraph interview. It is a necessary step in the intelligence business to bring new members into the club. It is a unique club where all of the members are highly trusted. You should be proud that you are being asked to join. I know that you have never taken a test like this before, and I know that most people are somewhat afraid of new experiences like this. Believe me, a lot of your fears will be relieved when you give me a chance to explain the process. I am going to explain everything to you in advance. Nothing will be done without your knowledge and permission. Absolutely nothing occurs during the process that will hurt you. There will be no surprises. You just need to settle down a little, listen to what I have to say, and proceed with the interview. The sooner we start, the sooner we'll finish, and the sooner you'll get a match for that cigarette. What do you say?"

He nervously listened to what I said and seemed to contemplate his options for a moment, but my words seemed to convince him to proceed. I walked him to the sitting room where I had the equipment positioned. Norma and Tom followed.

During my conduct of the pretest interview, his behavior changed little. He never stopped sucking on his unlit cigarette, and he continued to periodically interrupt me to ask permission to go find a match in the hotel lobby. He also continued some of the most bizarre fidgeting I had ever witnessed. Needless to say, his behavior was most peculiar.

Extreme nervousness should be treated by an examiner as a warning sign, a sign that something is wrong, perhaps seriously wrong. This is especially applicable when the nervousness is displayed by a foreign agent during the conduct of a clandestine examination conducted in his country. That evening, I didn't treat the warning sign as seriously as I should have. Perhaps I was anxious for Norma to see her first operational case using an interpreter. Perhaps my bloated stomach from all the scrumptious restaurant food affected my thinking, or maybe my can-do attitude interfered with my decision making. No matter the reason, the fact is that I tried to proceed with the agent's examination.

My plan for Norma to watch and learn pretty much went down the toilet. Shortly after I escorted the agent to the sitting room to begin the interview, Norma's stomach problems worsened, and she ran to the bathroom. I didn't see her for at least the next thirty minutes. I continued with the polygraph interview, and the agent continued with his Rodney Dangerfield impersonation. It should come as no surprise to learn that the initial charts I obtained were totally uninterpretable. The polygraph tracings were extremely erratic. The agent simply could not follow my directions to sit still during the collection of polygraph charts.

With charts in hand, I conferred with Tom in the adjoining room and told him that further testing would be futile. I advised I could either interrogate the agent under the assumption that his behavior was the result of practicing deception or that we could try again another day when the agent might be in a better mental state. Tom chose to terminate the session.

I returned to the agent and removed the polygraph attachments. He stood up and once again asked for permission to go to the lobby to search for some matches. The man had a one-track mind.

Turning to Tom, I said, "I want him to remain right here. I'll keep an eye on him. You go find him some matches while I finish packing up the instrument."

Tom left the suite and headed for the hotel lobby. I started to pack up the polygraph equipment in the sitting room, and the agent marched into the living room to begin pacing nervously back and forth. I watched him as he paced from the doorway of the sitting room to the far side of the living room, and then back again to the doorway of the sitting room. The agent continued to suck on his unlit cigarette as he paced. It was now a permanent fixture stuck between his lips.

Norma, still in the bathroom, did not have the slightest idea that the polygraph interview had been terminated. I felt terrible that the evening session, which was Norma's first opportunity to watch a covert case requiring an interpreter, had turned out to be a total waste of a training opportunity.

While I packed up the instrument in the sitting room, I tried to monitor the agent's pacing in the living room. Within a few minutes, I lost sight of him. I knew he did not go into the bathroom as it was obviously still occupied. A rush of concern overpowered me and I stopped packing up the instrument. I dashed into the living room and quickly saw that the agent was not there. A few more steps took me to the bedroom. Glancing in, I saw him sitting on the bed next to the nightstand with the telephone in his hand. A cold chill came over me as I realized that the worst-case scenario I had feared was unfolding before my very eyes. I rushed toward him to ask what he was doing. Before I could speak, I overheard him blurting out the hotel room number.

He said, *"Numero cinco quatro uno."*

I stammered out, *"Escuchame! Que pasa aqui?* [Listen! What's going on here?]"

The agent then slammed the phone down on the night-stand. He quickly stood up and charged straight at me. Bumping me aside with a hard shoulder like a football player, he ran out of the bedroom and through the living room, flung open the front door, and raced down the hall-way toward the elevators. In an instant, he was gone.

In polygraph school, students are taught to maintain control of an interview at all times. Instructors stress that the examiner is in charge and should be in total control of everything that transpires during the interview. It is the ex-aminer's room, and it is his equipment. The examiner is the expert. He controls the conversation, the questioning, and the interrogation. I was in control of very little that eve-ning as I stood all alone in the middle of the living room. It was quiet. I could hear my heart beating. The agent had fled the premises after contacting someone on the outside. He provided that person with the hotel room number. The case officer was also gone, off in search of a stupid match for the runaway agent. Norma was still busy in the bathroom, unaware that anything was wrong. As fear and worry set in, I chastised myself for not paying heed to the warning signs. A little self-flagellation was clearly in order.

Norma finally emerged from the bathroom as I stood all alone in the center of the living room. Time was of the essence so I quickly told her what had happened.

"Testing proved to be inconclusive due to the agent's nervousness. Tom elected to stop the interview. Tom left to find a match for the agent's cigarette. The agent got out of my sight. I caught him using the telephone in the bedroom. He divulged the hotel room number to someone and then ran out of here like a bat out of hell. Norma, this sounds really bad.

"I need your help getting the equipment packed up so we can get out of here as quickly as possible," I said. "If we don't leave soon, I think we might be arrested. We only have minutes."

As we busied ourselves with the instrument, the case officer returned to the room. I told him what had happened in his absence. His rosy complexion turned to a pale, ashen-gray color. He reached into his coat pocket, extracted a document, and blankly stared at it. I assume he was contemplating whether his documents would keep him out of jail. I walked over to a window in the sitting room that overlooked the front of the hotel and poked my head out to look down at the entrance. To my relief, I did not see any red flashing lights in the street below or hear any sirens in the distance. "Tom, we're leaving the polygraph in your care," I stated. "You seem to have some official documents. Maybe they will help. We're going to try to make it out of the hotel."

I pointed to a streetlight on the other side of the street directly across from the hotel's main entrance.

"If we're going to be arrested, I assume it will be in the hotel lobby or out front as we exit the hotel," I explained. "If you see us make it across the street to the streetlight, you can probably assume it is safe for you to leave."

Norma and I left Tom with the polygraph instrument in the hotel room and walked down the hall to the elevator. Hoping that the stairs would not empty out directly into the lobby, we decided to take the steps instead of the elevator. When we arrived at the lobby level, I quickly looked around for a back exit. Unable to locate one, we had no choice but to go through the lobby to exit through the front doors of the hotel. As we walked through the lobby, I glanced around looking for uniformed officers closing in on us. I prayed that the evening would not be a replay of what happened to a CIA officer in Asia many years before. He had also encountered an extremely nervous agent and hastily exited a hotel. A high-speed car chase ensued that ended with his arrest. The similarity of these events was alarming.

As we crossed the lobby, I gulped hard as I spied the agent standing next to the front doors. He glared at us as we approached him. I presumed he was there to point us out to the police or security service. I imagined him pointing at us while yelling, "That's them! Those are the American spies! Shoot them!"

Norma and I had no choice but to keep on walking toward the exit where the agent stood. Our options were very limited. The agent took several steps toward us as we neared the front doors, and I kept a wary eye on him, hoping that he would not produce a weapon. When he stopped in front of me, he apologized (in Spanish) and asked where Tom was. I understood what he said but had difficulty formulating a response in Spanish because the fight or flight syndrome had completely taken over my brain. My adrenaline was pumping and my mind was racing. I simply pointed up in the direction of the hotel room and rudely walked past him.

Norma and I made it safely across the street and paused under the streetlight so the case officer could see us from the window of the hotel room. We then took a rather convoluted, drawn-out route back to our hotel, making sure we were not being surveilled. We took a taxi to one area of the city, walked for a while, and then took another taxi to a different area of the city and walked again for several blocks. Finally, another taxi deposited us at a sidewalk café about ten blocks from our hotel. We ordered a cup of coffee and discussed the night's rather exciting events. It was well after midnight when we finally strolled back to our hotel. Needless to say and mildly put, the evening's activities had been rather exhilarating. I can only imagine what went through Norma's mind as she tried to drift off to sleep later that night. That was her first experience with covert operations polygraph testing in a foreign country. What an introductory case. I wouldn't have been surprised if she had hopped on the first plane home the next day.

There is a little more to this story of the runaway agent. Tom contacted the man the next day to find out what had disturbed him to the point he felt it necessary to flee the hotel room. The agent explained that he had called his wife to give her the room number because he was very frightened. He claimed he feared for his life, believing his polygraph examiner was going to kill him. Tom thought the agent's explanation was plausible. He managed to eventually soothe the man's fears and obtain his agreement to be retested during their next scheduled meeting. The office asked me to change my travel arrangements in order to stay a few more days to conduct the examination. I acquiesced after securing the agreement of the office in the next country I was scheduled to visit and ensuring I could make changes to my airline flights.

I didn't share the case officer's faith in the agent's story, so I wasn't surprised when the agent failed to show up for the next meeting. I was also not surprised when another of Polygraph Section's examiners tested and interrogated the agent about a year later and obtained admissions of having a secret relationship with the Russians. Unbeknownst to the case officer, the agent had been reporting to the Russians on all his contacts with his American case officer since the beginning of his "secret" relationship with us.

The agent had good reason to be extremely nervous during his polygraph session. Nervousness is normal, but his reaction was not normal. The polygraph process is an unwanted, scary endeavor for many who find themselves face-to-face with a "box man" and his intimidating equipment. Everyone who takes a polygraph test is nervous to one degree or another. The polygraph interview is simply one of those situations that people face in life that elicits a nervous response, and why should it not? First, it is an encounter that elicits a primordial fear—the fear of the unknown. When most people encounter a new or unknown situation, a nervous response arises and typically remains until the unknown aspects of the encounter subside. A polygraph examination is a new experience for most. People also experience nervousness when faced with situations that involve being interviewed and questioned by a stranger. People also tend to experience nervousness in testing situations. In addition, there are consequences to be paid for not doing well on a polygraph test. Consequences range from failing to get or losing a job, being denied a security clearance, having a security clearance revoked, or even facing criminal prosecution as the result of a bad test outcome.

I saw nervousness in examinees every day. However, when I saw nervousness that was clearly out of the ordinary, such as when an examinee was climbing the walls with fear, my self-preservation antennae would quickly go up. Whenever I encountered extreme nervousness in an examinee, it was probably not the result of the process being a new experience, or because it was an interview with a stranger, or because it was a testing situation. There was usually another more sinister reason for the nervousness. Extreme nervousness I encountered during a covert operations case in the field was probably a warning sign of impending danger.

I encountered this red flag of impending danger when I once traveled to a rather steamy Southeast Asian country to handle the examination of a Russian agent. The examination was one of several I conducted during my visit. The agent had been on the office's payroll for many years. She provided large amounts of information that had been disseminated throughout the intelligence community. However, her reporting was viewed as suspicious by analysts in Washington. For years, its veracity had been in doubt. Analysts questioned whether the agent had access to the individuals in the government she claimed to have. They felt her position was not important enough to give her access to the people who supposedly provided her with the information she passed to her case officer. Washington analysts openly speculated that she was being fed information by someone to provide to her American case officer. Some of the information she had provided had been corroborated through other sources, but there were significant portions of her information that had been unsubstantiated.

There had been at least two previous attempts over the years to have her submit to a polygraph examination. Both attempts failed. When her case officer, John, broached the polygraph requirement with her on those occasions, she agreed to be polygraphed, but with great trepidation. In an attempt to assuage her fears, John alerted her in advance of each scheduled examination so she would not be surprised by the looming polygraph. She failed to appear for each of those meetings with her case officer and thus avoided the polygraph tests. Of course, this displeased and worried both John and Headquarters, so having the agent submit to the polygraph process became a priority.

When I arrived in country, John told me that he had changed his strategy. This time he wasn't going to tell the agent in advance of the impending polygraph test. Instead, he planned to surprise her with my "unexpected" arrival in town and spring the test on her as a last-minute decision to take advantage of my presence.

On the day of the polygraph examination, John rented a suite in a luxurious hotel. I set up the polygraph equipment in a backroom so the agent wouldn't be frightened by its presence during our initial introductions and discussions. John asked me to take the lead in getting her to agree to take the polygraph test.

After John brought the agent to the hotel room, I was introduced as a security officer from Washington, and we all sat down in the living room. The agent's nervousness was quite obvious. My presence, something that was unexpected and not at all typical of their usual meetings, obviously disturbed the agent. Once she discovered that I was a polygraph examiner from Washington, her nervousness increased two-fold. Perhaps "nervousness" is a poor word to describe her condition. "Fear," or perhaps "terror" would be better words to use. I talked to the agent about the benefits of taking the polygraph examination, such as making herself more valuable to us and implying, but not actually offering, increased pay.

"You'll become one of the trusted members of the inner circle," I said. "I have traveled from Washington DC specifically for your examination because Washington has found your information to be of great value. You should feel very proud, and you should also be honored that your contribution is so valuable that you are being asked to join the club. The polygraph test is part of your initiation. We all take the test. You aren't being asked to go through anything we haven't gone through ourselves."

I let her know that I was prepared to guide her through the process. I described the way the polygraph interview would be conducted from beginning to end and provided her with an explanation of the instrument, its components, and the sensors. Unexpectedly, the more I talked, the more nervous and fearful she became. On rare occasions, an overview may not appreciably reduce an examinee's level of nervousness, but it certainly should not invoke stark terror. My self-preservation antennae should have gone up at that point, but they did not. I was too preoccupied with my attempts to gain her trust, assuage her fears, and secure her agreement to undergo polygraph testing. Her fear and resistance proved to be a challenge for my powers of persuasion. I must have been persuasive enough though, because I did eventually manage to secure her agreement.

The entire interview up to that point had been conducted in the living room, deliberately out of sight of the intimidating polygraph equipment. I advised the agent that the next step in the polygraph interview process was to move to the backroom of the hotel suite where I had the polygraph instrument assembled and ready for use. Hearing that statement, she visibly shook with fear. Her hands and arms trembled and her lips quivered. She was absolutely terrified. She nervously glanced in the direction of the backroom and made attempts to rise out of her chair but seemed to be unable to actually stand up. When she finally mustered enough courage or strength to rise, she did so slowly and shakily. As she stood up and turned toward the backroom, I noticed a huge yellow puddle in her chair. She had been so terrified while sitting in her chair that she lost control of her bladder as I talked with her. I glanced quickly at John and noticed him staring at the yellow puddle. We briefly exchanged surprised looks, but I turned away from John and followed the agent into the backroom.

As I continued the polygraph interview in the backroom, her nervousness never subsided, and she never settled down to the point that I felt she would be a suitable subject for testing. Nevertheless, I had little choice but to try to proceed. The interview progressed to the point of trying to obtain polygraph charts, but as expected, the charts I obtained were completely erratic and uninterpretable. I conferred with the case officer over the test results and advised that we had two courses of action. The first was to assume that the agent was being deceptive to one or more of the test issues and to interrogate her. The second was to retest again in the future, with the hope that her fear would be less next time now that she had been exposed to the process. I did not argue for very long when the case officer stated he wanted to terminate the session. At the time, I felt her irrational fears of the polygraph process were the cause of the inconclusive charts I obtained. Terminating the interview seemed like the most compassionate and humane decision at the time.

Weeks later, when I discussed the case with a senior examiner at my regional office, he was greatly disappointed that I had not tried harder to overcome the case officer's decision to terminate the session. He thought I made a terrible mistake by not convincing him to take the opportunity to interrogate the agent. He had read her files and was prepared to conduct the case during one of the previous unsuccessful attempts to polygraph her, and he thought I should have interrogated her. He firmly believed that all of the suspicions expressed by Washington's analysts were well founded and that her fears of the polygraph test were based on a fear of being detected as providing us with false information for years.

The examiner got a second chance to polygraph the agent about a year later. After a rather lengthy and persistent interrogation, his session with her resulted in significant admissions of working against her American case officer at the direction of the Russians. She had been providing us false information, mixed in with some innocuous, true information, at their direction for years.

There is one final little episode to this story about the agent and her yellow puddle. When I returned home at the end of the trip, my wife asked me whether I enjoyed my travel to the country.

"It was great." I told her. "I met a blonde Russian woman one night—a tall, slim, attractive gal. I took her to the bedroom of a swank hotel suite, and she got so excited about what I was going to do to her that she trembled in anticipation and wet her undies. But don't worry. It was official business."

My wife simply said, "You sure picked a strange way to make a living."

No argument here!

Chapter Twelve

Castro's Buddy Beats the Box

It is hard to believe that a man is telling the
truth when you know that you would lie if you
were in his place.

—H. L. MENCKEN

I know that extreme nervousness displayed by
a polygraph subject during an operational case can
be a warning sign that connotes impending danger.
I am accustomed to encountering nervousness; however, it
is a difficult task to determine when the examinee's behavior has crossed the line and become something out of
the ordinary, something that would be considered to be
extreme nervousness. Of course, if I become aware of it in
the midst of a clandestine meeting, it may already be too
late. I could already be in the crosshairs of the host coun-

try's intelligence service and may have walked right into a trap they set.

The exact opposite of extreme nervousness can also be a warning sign. An examinee that approaches the polygraph process with an abundance of self-confidence can be a pleasure to test. If he is self-assured, confident, and free of the general nervous tension that I too often saw, polygraph testing can be a swift and straightforward process. On the other hand, an overly self-confident agent should also be a warning sign.

One week before Christmas in the mid-1970s, Cuban Ops (the Directorate of Operations office handling the Cuban target) contacted Polygraph Section with an urgent request to test one of their agents in a small city in Europe. The agent had been previously polygraphed with favorable results on two occasions. I knew that both examiners who had previously tested the agent had solid reputations as thorough, competent examiners. However, the test I was asked to conduct was requested for special reasons. The examination was of critical importance because the Agency thought it had caught the agent contacting the head of the DGI (*Dirección General de Inteligencia*), the Cuban Intelligence Service, in another city in Europe. The official decision on the identity of the individual was deemed "Inconclusive," but Headquarters officers were almost positive it was our agent. There were also other aspects of the agent's relationship with us, including the authenticity of his reporting, that officers at Headquarters deemed suspicious. For example, the agent had provided a diagram of a room where the Agency was considering to surreptitiously place a piece of electronic equipment. They thought the diagram was so good, perhaps even professionally drawn, that he must have had help.

The previous tests were arranged and administered when the agent left Cuba to attend conferences in foreign countries. On those occasions, he traveled with a group, but was able to break away for a sufficient amount of time to meet with a case officer. Just as he had managed before, the agent anticipated being able to sneak away from his group of fellow travelers for a few hours on December 22 while on his current business trip to several European countries.

Making travel arrangements on such short notice only one week before Christmas meant there was but a slim chance of booking a return flight from Europe to be home on December 25. When word of the polygraph requirement spread through the office, the senior examiners brought out their best excuses or were nowhere to be found. Christmas was the one holiday of the year that no examiner wanted to miss. Nevertheless, the office had to select an examiner quickly. Frankly, it never occurred to me to hide or make an excuse. After all, this was a trip to Europe. I could say that I was chosen above all others in the office because of my proven abilities to successfully resolve the most difficult of polygraph cases, or because I was the "go to" examiner whenever the impossible needed to be done, but I won't. Nonetheless, I was chosen to the great relief of many other examiners, and I successfully made travel arrangements. I obtained confirmed reservations that allowed me to arrive at the European city on time, but my return flight was left open. My ability to return in time for Christmas was entirely dependent on whether the agent was available for polygraph testing during his conference as was anticipated.

My travel from Washington DC to the European city was uneventful. I was met at the airport by two case officers, both of whom were also on TDY from Headquarters. They drove me to my hotel, made sure I got settled in, and gave me instructions for meeting them the next day at the office.

I knew that polygraph equipment was not normally stored at this office and that our examiner stationed in another European country had shipped equipment for me to use for this rather important case. One of my first orders of business at the office the next day was to make sure the equipment he sent was in good operating condition. I asked about the location of the equipment and was pointed in the direction of a storage closet. I searched for quite a while but was unable to locate the equipment. Of course, I was looking for our standard equipment—a Stoelting, Executive Model, three-channel, battery-powered, community inkwell polygraph instrument built into a briefcase. A helpful support officer pointed to a big, gray metal box on the top shelf. I took the metal box off the shelf, opened its top, and saw that it was an ancient Keeler polygraph instrument. I had seen pictures of such an instrument, and I think our office at Headquarters had one in the storage room, but I certainly had never used one. My inspection of this antiquated equipment revealed a community inkwell system

unlike anything I had seen before. I was surprised to discover that its pneumograph tube was about six times as big
as the one used with a modern Stoelting instrument, and
I was even more surprised to find a galvanic skin response
bar that had to be held in the palm of the hand with a
watchband used to hold it in place. It appeared to be jury-
rigged. I was accustomed to finger plates that were held on
by Velcro straps on the fingertips. The coup de grâce of my
equipment inspection was a blood pressure cuff that un-
rolled to an extraordinary length of seven feet or so. There
was no Velcro on the cuff, and there were no snaps or hooks
to secure the cuff after it was wrapped around the arm. After some fumbling on my own arm, I finally deduced that
one must wrap the cuff around the arm, over and over again,
and then tuck the end in to hold it in place. In any case,
although I had no training or experience with the "dino-
saur" equipment, I was able to get it all figured out and in
good operating condition.

After inspecting the polygraph equipment and making
all other necessary preparations with the case officers, by
midday the three of us got settled into a hotel room to be
used for the polygraph interview. We waited nine or ten
hours for the agent to make contact. Suffering through a
long and boring wait, I was virtually certain he was going
to be a no-show. I would have put money on it at the time,
but at last he followed through with his contact instructions. One of the case officers left to meet him somewhere
in the city to bring him back to the hotel room.

From the very moment we were introduced, I realized

that the man was one of the most self-confident individuals I ever met. He was an impressive person who was full of bravado and machismo. Confidence flowed from everything he did and said. There was nothing hesitant about the man and there were certainly no indications at all that he was nervous. I thought, *If I found myself in a hotel room with three foreign intelligence officers, I'd sure be nervous.* As far as I could tell, he appeared to be supremely self-assured. You could see it in the way he moved and hear it in the way he spoke. I was very impressed, but I set my personal impressions aside to conduct an impartial, unbiased polygraph interview.

I conducted a very thorough polygraph interview and examination. I administered several different types of polygraph examinations that covered Headquarters' concerns, and the agent passed each test with flying colors. I administered a test with questions about false reporting and revealing his relationship with us to any unauthorized people, as well as a test designed to determine whether he had been in contact with the Cuban Intelligence Service. The results were clearly not deceptive. Finally, I challenged him on the quality of the diagram that Headquarters felt must have been created by a professional. He laughed when I told him of Headquarters' concern.

"Please, give me a piece of paper and a pencil," he demanded.

One of the case officers fulfilled his request, and the agent then proceeded to draw the diagram from memory. When he was finished, he passed it to the three of us. Since

I had just seen the original at Headquarters a few days earlier, I was able to mentally compare the two. His latest rendition looked superb to me, certainly better than I could have done.

The agent boasted, "If Headquarters is so impressed with the professional quality of my diagram, perhaps I should ask for a raise."

He laughed heartily at his own witticism. Everything about the man was impressive. Subsequent polygraph testing clearly supported his statement that he had received no assistance in drawing the original diagram he provided his Agency contact.

In defiance of the odds and to the dismay of those back at my office who placed bets on whether I would return in time for Christmas, I made it back to Washington on December 24. Shortly after I got settled in at home to make final arrangements for Christmas, I received a phone call from the office. I was ordered to come to Headquarters to brief a gathering of Cuban Ops officers on the results of my session with the agent. Even though it was Christmas Eve, I made my way to Headquarters and provided them with the details of my debriefing of the agent, my impression of the agent and his comportment during the interview, a description of the various polygraph examinations I conducted to address their concerns, and the favorable results of all the tests conducted. I was unable to provide them with an explanation for the contact with DGI they were almost certain was made by the agent. I explained I was absolutely confident in the results I had obtained during testing. Not hearing the news they expected, they were not happy with anything I said. They had been (and still were) almost positive that the agent was the individual caught contacting the DGI.

One officer said to me, "It's simple. He beat you."

"The possibility of getting beaten during a polygraph examination is always there, but I don't think that possibility is very strong in this case because the polygraph results are so clearly and unmistakably nondeceptive. I am as sure as I can be," I replied.

Based on the agent's history of successfully completing previous polygraph examinations, on my assessment of his behavior, on my assessment of his responses to debriefing questions, and on my evaluation of his polygraph test results, I was confident in my analysis and with the final call of No Deception Indicated.

There is an unexpected and bitter ending to this story. In a most unfortunate turn of events, about two years later I was advised that Fidel Castro had been seen on Cuban television with his arm around the shoulders of the agent I tested. Castro revealed to the world that my examinee had been a double agent against American intelligence for many years. As you would expect, Polygraph Section was asked to do a damage assessment review of the case. Fortunately for me, they arrived at the same No Deception Indicated decision during their review, meaning I did not make a mistake in chart interpretation for the tests I had conducted. Looking back now, I'm not surprised that the agent lacked the fear of detection necessary for the polygraph process to work. After all, he also beat the two previous examiners who had tested him. His previous success in beating the polygraph process did nothing but bolster his confidence during my session with him—and he already had an overabundance of confidence.

As a result of that case, I learned the lesson that not only nervousness, but also the lack of nervousness can be important clues for a field examiner. General nervous tension is normal. Extreme nervousness is not normal and may be a warning sign for the examiner. An examiner faced with such an examinee should be very wary. On the other hand, a self-confident examinee can be a joy to work with, but an overly self-confident examinee can also be another type of subject a field examiner should be suspicious of, as I now know only too well.

Chapter Thirteen

Mata Hari

All men are born truthful and die liars.
—MARQUIS DE VAUVENARGUES

ll examinees would like nothing better than to have their polygraph examinations end with favorable outcomes. I don't believe that examinees submit to the process wanting to get caught if they are trying to conceal information. In the same vein, I don't believe examinees want to be erroneously identified as being deceptive if they are telling the truth. Some have faith in the process, trust their examiner, and decide to simply cooperate with the situation to the fullest extent possible. They follow their examiner's instructions and answer all the examiner's questions honestly and completely. Others don't have faith in the process and have little confidence in their examiner. Some try to influence the outcome of the examination to make sure the examiner correctly classifies them as truth tellers, while others will do the same in an attempt to keep an examiner from correctly identifying their lies.

The decisions that polygraph examiners make can sometimes be influenced by outside factors such as illness and fatigue. Examiners may cut interrogations short or overlook consistency in responses in charts if they are not mentally sharp. Monitoring their cases and requiring a quality control review of their work can catch any errors due to such influence. In addition, people who have a vested interest in the outcome of someone's test may attempt to influence an examiner's decision. Examiners may be wined and dined by case officers or office chiefs in subtle attempts to influence. Examiners may even be the recipients of unabashed, brazen pressure to arrive at certain test results.

There is another type of external manipulation of a polygraph examiner that is sometimes used to try to influence the decision-making process. Sexual influence is attempted by both men and women. Male examinees try to employ masculine charm to sway a female examiner's decisions, and female examinees try to use their feminine wiles to influence male examiners. I don't believe this happens very frequently in the polygraph setting, but I've personally experienced it on a number of occasions. Usually, attempts are rather subtle and flirtatious in nature, such as when women make use of a raised skirt, a twinkle in the

eye, a giggle, a smile, a compliment, or an expressed interest in the examiner. Occasionally, it is much more direct.

One examiner at Headquarters conducted an examination of a rather attractive female examinee and obtained
unmistakably deceptive reactions to one of the test questions. During posttest interrogation the examiner stated,
"Your test results clearly show that you haven't told me the
truth. You consistently responded to this question for reasons that you've decided to not share with me. You are
clearly concerned about your answer to the question, and
you are clearly withholding your thoughts and concerns
from me."

The examinee batted her eyelashes, smiled, and responded to the examiner in a very sultry, seductive tone,
"You're absolutely right. I've had some very strong and very
personal thoughts during the test. I must tell you that I find
you incredibly handsome. I've been sexually attracted to you
since we met. Throughout the test, I had naughty thoughts
of making love to you."

Her attempts to influence the examiner did not work.
Subsequent admissions of extensive illegal drug use prevented her from being granted a security clearance.

Most attempts to influence examiners were subtle in nature, but some were very direct, open, and obvious like the
example above. A fellow male examiner once told me of a
verbal exchange with a polygraph examinee that was almost
identical to the one above, except that the examinee was
also male. Needless to say, once word spread around the

office, the teasing inflicted upon him by his fellow examiners was unrelenting.

I once conducted the polygraph examination of a female industrial contractor in the 1970s. Being the highly trained and skilled investigator that I was, when I met her in the reception room I was quick to observe that she was braless. Nothing gets past my powers of observation. Then again, her see-through blouse removed any doubt that anyone would possibly have. I deduced that it was either the chill of the air conditioning or my male charisma that made her nipples stand at attention. It was probably the chill. Was she making a fashion statement, or was she attempting to influence the outcome of her examination? Unfortunately, she attempted to lie during her examination on the issue of illegal drug use. During subsequent interrogation, she admitted quite extensive use of illegal drugs, and I am sure that the amount, frequency, and recency of her drug use led to the denial of a security clearance. While I may have been both distracted and impressed by her blatantly visible attributes during the interview, I can safely say that I didn't allow her appearance to influence my handling of the case, and I certainly did not unnecessarily prolong the interview. At least that's my story, and I'm sticking to it. After all, it would take more than a braless examinee in a see-through blouse to divert me from my mission of fighting for truth, justice, and the American way.

Although the case of the braless examinee was certainly memorable, it is not my best example of feminine wiles directed against me. That honor goes to a case I conducted in a city in the Far East. A case officer had recruited a female American citizen to be utilized by the office in a support capacity. The office planned to utilize her apartment as a safe house. They also planned to have mail delivered to her address and have her responsible for delivering that mail to the case officer. The case was a simple one in the sense that it more closely resembled an applicant case conducted at Headquarters than a covert operations case of a foreign national. My review of the information in her file revealed that she was a young lady who attended school while working part-time. She was a social contact of the case officer.

On the evening of the examination, the case officer escorted me to the hotel room he had secured for the conduct of the polygraph interview. I set up the polygraph equipment in the room, and the case officer departed to meet with the young lady in the hotel lobby. Since she was an American citizen, not only was the case officer's presence during the interview not needed, it was not permitted due to privacy concerns. When he met her in the lobby, he simply gave her the room number and told her that Mr. Johnson was waiting to conduct her polygraph interview.

After waiting in the hotel room for a short while, I heard a knock on the door. Expecting the arrival of the examinee, Ms. Jones, I walked over to the door, opened it, and found myself face-to-face with a breathtakingly beautiful young woman standing in the doorway. I looked at her with an admiring eye. Before me stood a young lady who could have been a movie star or an internationally famous supermodel. Her beauty was the type that makes a young man act silly and an old man weep in remembrance of better days. Her striking figure was nicely packaged in a tight red dress and black high-heeled shoes. She had long, blonde hair with a slight curl that caressed her bare shoulders, and she had a wonderfully warm smile. I was taken aback by her good looks, and I'm sure it showed in my behavior before I could regain my composure. For an instant, I must have looked at her like a starving man looks at a piece of cooking meat, but I quickly recovered and reverted back to acting the role of the consummate security professional. That sly case officer should have given me some warning.

With a perky, warm smile and a twinkle in her eye, she extended her hand and asked, "Mr. Johnson?"

"Yes. Ms. Jones? Come in," I answered.

Ms. Jones entered, and I proceeded to conduct the polygraph interview exactly as I would conduct any other. I tried my best to ignore her beauty. She comported herself in a way I would expect someone with such beauty to behave. Perhaps unconsciously, she used her beauty to her advantage, although in a subtle manner. She was very friendly, very polite, and she smiled and posed a lot. At the time, I thought her behavior was only mildly flirtatious and that she was merely accustomed to using her attributes to her advantage. In fact, I even thought my interpretation of her behavior might be a figment of my overactive imagination with a dash of wishful thinking thrown in. After all, all men are prone to live in a bit of a Walter Mitty fantasy world from time to time.

The polygraph interview progressed without difficulty. She followed my directions, cooperated, answered truthfully, and eventually completed the examination without any indications of deception and without providing any information that would have a negative impact on the office's plans for her. At the end of interview, I removed the polygraph sensors and advised her that she had successfully completed the test. I thanked her for her cooperation and told her she was free to leave and enjoy the rest of her evening. I stated I had to pack up the polygraph equipment and would be leaving the room soon after her.

Ms. Jones was not in a hurry to leave. She rose out of the chair she had been sitting in, crossed the room, and sat down on the edge of the bed. She slowly crossed her long legs.

She said, "Mr. Johnson, what a fascinating experience that was. How exciting to take a real polygraph test in a hotel room here in the city. It's all done so secretly, too. I'll bet that Johnson isn't even your real name. You were so good at handling my polygraph test. Have you been doing this type of work for long?"

"Yes. Quite a few years," I replied.

"You lucky, lucky man," she said. "No wonder you're so good. Do you get to travel to other countries?"

"Well, yes," I replied. "I've traveled to many countries of the world to conduct polygraph tests."

"You must have lots and lots of stories to tell. Oh, the experiences you must have had. How fascinating. What a wonderful life you must lead. I'm so jealous and so envious of you," she said.

Her eyes looked deep into mine as she spoke, and the tone of her voice seemed to lower. There was a husky, sultry undertone in her voice. Also, as she talked, she leaned back on the bed until she was on her elbows, almost lying down. Her short skirt rose dangerously high. She smiled warmly. Was this my overactive imagination running wild or was her behavior actually suggestive?

"Yes, I agree. I think this is an exciting way to make a living. I've traveled to many exotic lands, seen much of the world, and I'm sure I have quite a few stories I could tell about conducting polygraph examinations," I said.

I turned and started to gather the polygraph sensors together in preparation for packing up the instrument. Ms. Jones sat up, stood up, and walked over to me.

"Mr. Johnson, before you close up that briefcase, will you please show me how this works? It's just so fascinating, and you seem to be so good at what you do. I'm very curious" she said.

"Well, I guess I can give you a quick demo and explanation. I know the instrument looks complicated, but it's really very simple," I said.

"What's that mahoozit?" she asked.

"That? Oh, that's a sphygmomanometer, a blood pressure meter," I replied.

I proceeded to describe the various components of the

instrument and gave a quick demonstration of how a polygraph chart is produced and interpreted. As I bent over the instrument to point at its parts, turn dials, and produce a short chart with some red squiggly lines on it, Ms. Jones stood behind me, leaned over, and placed her hands on my shoulders. As she bent forward to watch over my shoulder, I could feel her press lightly against my back. Her head lowered until it was right next to mine and her hair dangled against my neck. Her long blonde hair tickled my neck, and I instantly broke out in goose bumps.

Heavy breathing emanated from her lips, which were only an inch from my left ear. Like the sex kittens portrayed by the film industry, she purred in my ear, "Mr. Johnson, I get tingly all over when you talk about polygraph. This is all so fascinating. I could listen to you all night long. All night long."

Men are probably genetically programmed with an automatic response to such blatant overtures by extremely attractive members of the opposite sex, and we've had centuries of practice letting that programming take hold. Her behavior was not a figment of my overactive imagination. Her behavior exceeded anything I had imagined.

Although we hadn't parted ways, the polygraph interview was over. She had been informed that the interview was over and that she had successfully resolved all the issues covered in her polygraph examination. Therefore, she wasn't using her feminine wiles to try to influence the outcome of the test. She was trying to seduce me.

I realized that the polygraph examiner's Code of

Ethics did not specifically cover such a situation. There was nothing written that said, "Thou shalt not engage in sexual activity with an examinee in the examination room directly following a polygraph interview." There was a directive that said, "A member shall respect the rights and dignity of all persons to whom they administer polygraph examinations." It seemed to me that if anyone's rights and dignity were not being respected, they were mine. Ms. Jones was the evil seductress. I was the prey. Then there was the directive that said, "A member shall not solicit or accept fees, gratuities, or gifts that are intended to influence his or her opinion, decision, or report." Since the polygraph interview was over, the gratuities she seemed to be offering couldn't be an effort on her part to influence my opinion, decision, or report.

Code of Ethics or not, her intentions, as delightfully arousing as they were, made me extremely ill at ease. I was suspicious of some ulterior motive driving those intentions of hers, and I realized that I simply couldn't follow through with anything she had in mind. Traveling around the world as I did, she certainly wasn't the first to throw temptation my way. However, I was not accustomed to getting sexual approaches from examinees that looked like international supermodels with the morals of an alley cat in heat. Fortunately, I was clearheaded enough to realize neither my wife nor my office would consider it to be appropriate, professional behavior.

I stood up and moved several paces away from Ms. Jones, extracting myself from her suggestive purring in my ear. I prompted her to leave the hotel room by suggesting that I had to finish packing up the equipment to conduct another examination elsewhere in the city that evening. I lied. At least that evening didn't turn out to be one of those occasions when I made an incredibly stupid decision.

Yes, women sometimes try to use their feminine wiles to try to influence the outcome of polygraph examinations. I am aware that polygraph examiners have dated examinees and have even married examinees. This case is the only one I am aware of involving an examinee attempting to seduce an examiner in the exam room immediately following an interview that concluded with No Deception Indicated results.

Chapter Fourteen

A Failure to Communicate

Truth is mighty and will prevail. There is
nothing the matter with this, except that it
ain't so.

—MARK TWAIN

W hen the Agency included the use of the
polygraph as a tool in the agent authentication process in 1948, a love-hate relationship between case
officers and polygraph examiners began. Case officers spend
many long hours spotting, assessing, developing, recruiting, training, and handling agents. These steps in the recruitment process may take weeks, or even years. It can be
dangerous. It can involve many uncompensated hours of
work. Recruiting and handling valuable, productive agents
can lead to awards and promotions for case officers. Repu-

tations can be made that can be career enhancing. A great deal of professional and emotional investment by a case officer goes into developing an agent.

The use of polygraph testing in the agent validation process is not a requirement. The polygraph is a tool available for their use. When a polygraph examiner tests an agent and provides a case officer with a No Deception Indicated (NDI) test result, everyone is happy. The case officer is happy because it means his initial assessment of the agent and the veracity of the agent's reporting had been correct, and his relationship with the agent will continue. The agent is happy because he gets a clean bill of health, continues in the working relationship, and continues to get paid. The polygraph examiner is happy because an NDI test usually means an easier, shorter test, and an easier report to write.

On the other hand, when the result of an agent's test is Deception Indicated (DI), there are fewer happy people. The examiner may have obtained admissions of revealing the secret relationship to unauthorized people, of working for another intelligence service (perhaps even against us), or of falsifying information provided to the case officer. A polygraph examiner's "success" in uncovering derogatory information is sometimes perceived as the case officer's "failure." In some cases, the case officer may have spent years of his life handling an agent, only to have a polygraph examination of several hours' duration put an end to the operation.

I have suspected case officers of hiding their agents from visiting polygraph examiners at times. On a number of occasions I have seen an examiner arrive at a CIA office with several cases on his agenda, only to have the remaining agents suddenly become unavailable after the first case conducted resulted in a DI call. I am sure some of those "no shows" were legitimate, but I am also sure that some were the result of efforts on the part of the case officers to protect their agents and prolong their operations. As a polygraph examiner, I could probably be accused of having an overabundance of suspicion and skepticism, but I prefer to think of it instead as a rather realistic understanding of human nature.

Despite the love-hate relationship, communication between the polygraph examiner and the case officer is just as important as communication between the examiner and the agent. The administration of a polygraph examination may be just another routine activity for the examiner, something he does almost every day, if not twice a day, but that "routine" examination for the agent and the case officer may be one of the most important events in their lives. Both have a great deal at stake. A polygraph examination for them is anything but "routine." I have seen a number of examiners forget this and treat test results in a clinical or seemingly uncaring manner. As a result they probably added fuel to the fire. Even worse, I have seen some examiners get excited and joyful after obtaining damaging admissions from an agent as the result of posttest interrogation. You could equate this behavior with a doctor's poor bedside manner. Imagine a doctor excitedly telling a husband, "After my exhaustive investigation and testing I've discovered your wife has cancer! A job well done I'd say, right?"

As vital as good communication is between the examiner, the case officer, and the agent, it is unfortunate that unintentional misinterpretations or misunderstandings occur every now and then as they communicate. There was a case officer, Bill, in the Latin America office who will probably hate me for the rest of his life because of a misunderstanding. It started with the conduct of a routine polygraph examination of one of his agents in a South American country. I didn't conduct the test myself. I accompanied another examiner, Frank, who was on his first overseas trip. The case was but one of many we handled for the office during our visit.

Preparation for the examination went by the book. Frank conferred with Bill in advance and checked on the security of the meeting arrangements. Frank reviewed the file at the office, prepared the questions to be used during the test, and reviewed the questions with Bill. Bill told Frank that the agent was a very pleasant fellow who was friendly and easy to work with. He enjoyed their routine meetings. He also said the agent graciously accepted the requirement to take a polygraph test. Bill thought we would have a very short, trouble-free polygraph session.

On the day of the examination, Bill escorted both of us to a safe house. It was an apartment that had all the necessary furniture for conducting the interview. Bill departed to meet with the agent at some not too distant location and escort him to the apartment. We began to set up the polygraph equipment in a backroom. When Bill and the agent returned, it did not take long to learn that the case officer had been correct in his assessment of the agent's demeanor. He was a friendly, happy man who seemed to enjoy his association with the Americans. He was certainly a most pleasant fellow, just as Bill had described. He spoke English, so Bill was not needed as an interpreter. He remained in the living room as we moved to the backroom to conduct the polygraph interview.

But testing didn't go well for the agent. After our analysis of the polygraph charts resulted in a clear DI call, Frank and I went out to the living room to brief Bill on the test results. He was quite surprised. It probably never entered his mind that his jovial agent would have difficulty with a polygraph examination. Frank explained that only the agent knew the reason for his consistently deceptive reactions to the relevant questions during testing and that the next course of action should be to interrogate in order to discover the reason. Bill consented to the interrogation, feeling that it was imperative to resolve the problematic issues.

The interrogation was lengthy and persistent, but ultimately nonproductive. Frank did an excellent job. He questioned, probed, queried, and challenged. He provided many rational arguments as to why it would be in the agent's best interest to resolve the issues. He was persuasive, sympathetic, and understanding, but he was unsuccessful. The agent continued to be a pleasant fellow during persistent questioning, but he stuck to his story like a broken record.

He claimed he had no idea why he repeatedly reacted to questions about revealing his secret relationship to unauthorized people and reporting false information to Bill.

Frank needed additional information from the agent in order to continue the examination. Once obtained, he could conduct more tests to verify the agent was no longer withholding information on the test issues.

Unfortunately, the agent provided no reasonable explanation for his reactions on the test during hours of interrogation. Frank decided to brief the case officer on the status of the interview once again. We both met with Bill in the living room and advised him that no significant information had been obtained during the questioning of the agent and that he hadn't provided any reasonable explanation for his reactions. We also advised him that no additional tests could be conducted, but that the examiner could continue interrogating if Bill so desired. I noticed Bill look at his watch and could tell he was not keen on the idea of continuing the interrogation. We advised that the interview could be concluded now with DI results, allowing Bill to continue trying to persuade the agent to reveal his concerns during future meetings. This option had some degree of success in other cases in the past. Agents sometimes felt more comfortable with their case officers because bonds of friendship had been established. When their concerns dealt with some type of minor indiscretion, they might be more open to confiding in their case officer. Bill asked us to end the interview.

The interview was terminated. As we closed out the

session, the agent continued to be his good-humored self. He engaged us all in conversation on various topics and obviously had a cheerful, upbeat attitude about life in general. Setting the agent's negative test results to one side for a moment, I thought he was simply a pleasant person to be around. After the agent departed, the three of us decided to get something to eat. Bill recommended a steakhouse restaurant that was only several blocks away. We decided to walk there.

During our walk to the restaurant, the miscommunication began with an innocent-sounding question from Bill.

"What do you think of my guy?" he asked.

Both of us provided him with our observation that the agent seemed to be a marvelous person. We made remarks about how friendly he was, how outgoing he seemed to be, and what a buoyant personality he had. Bill beamed and agreed with us. For the rest of the walk to the restaurant, we listened to Bill talk about how wonderful the agent was and how much he enjoyed meeting with the man.

Lunch was absolutely fantastic. Bill made an outstanding restaurant choice, a scrumptious Brazilian steakhouse. Later that afternoon at the office, Frank worked on the draft of his report of the polygraph interview. I reviewed and approved it. Frank then put the report in the appropriate format to be reviewed and released by the responsible office personnel.

When we arrived at the office the next morning we were immediately cornered by the case officer. He must have been lying in wait to pounce on us as soon as we entered the office. He was so livid that he could barely hold himself back from striking one of us. He accused us of stabbing him in the back by changing the final call of the polygraph examination of his agent to DI. As calmly as we could under his tirade, we explained that the results were DI and had always been DI.

He said, "I asked you both what you thought of my guy and you said he was fine, he was nice, he was wonderful."

I said, "That had nothing to do with the polygraph results."

Bill complained that he specifically asked us how things went. I tried once again to explain that the agent was indeed a fine, pleasant man, but that the polygraph results were clearly DI and that is what we told him at the safe house. He would not accept that and was obviously convinced that we were pulling a fast one on him for some reason.

We couldn't convince him he misconstrued our comments about the agent's personality as comments about the polygraph results. He turned his back on us and stormed into the chief's office for a closed-door meeting. After a while we were summoned by the chief.

At the chief's request, Frank described the chain of events and conversations that led to the case officer's misunderstanding. The chief listened and then probably formed his own opinion based on what he heard from the case officer as well as from Frank's description of the events. Nevertheless, the chief was left with two unpleasant facts. First, he had an irate case officer on his hands who felt he had been wronged; and second, he had DI polygraph results on an agent case that could result in termination of the agent. He thought for a moment and then asked me, as the senior examiner, to retest the agent. I thought it over for a moment and then flatly refused.

"If the accuracy or validity of the polygraph test was at all in doubt, I would be happy to retest the agent," I said. "But I sat in on the polygraph examination from start to finish. I observed Frank the entire time. He conducted that examination in a thoroughly competent and professional manner, and I am in one hundred percent agreement with his analysis. The case clearly resulted in a DI call, and the examiner's report is entirely accurate. There is absolutely no reason to retest the agent on the same issues."

I explained that I could continue the interrogation and then perhaps do more testing if admissions were obtained or plausible explanations were provided, but that I couldn't ethically retest on the same questions. The chief, who may have outranked me by three or four grades, didn't like my response. He tried to intimidate me into doing the test again. I believe he understood the logic of my position and heard the firmness and conviction in my voice. I think he was putting on a show for the sake of his relationship with the case officer. I flatly refused to retest the agent on the same test questions, the chief let it drop, and the case officer stormed out of the office in anger.

I'll never understand how the case officer so misconstrued our words. I can only conclude it was a case of selective hearing; he heard what he so strongly wanted to believe. In any event, he did not speak to us after that day, and I assume he could be telling his story of his encounter with the two backstabbing, deceitful polygraph examiners to this day.

Fortunately, an encounter of this type is rare, but unfortunately, I've experienced such pressure on several occasions. I vividly recollect another incident that occurred after I had returned to the office in a different Central American city, I believe, following the conduct of a polygraph examination that had concluded with a DI call. I was busy working on the draft of the final polygraph report when I was summoned to the chief's office. I entered and saw that the case officer for the examination I had just completed was sitting next to the chief. The chief asked me to recount the details of the polygraph session, so I gave an account of how the interview and interrogation progressed and how the session ended.

"Alan, how sure are you about the polygraph results?" he asked after listening to what I had to say.

"I'm one hundred percent confident with my analysis of the charts," I replied. "Why?"

"Wouldn't it be prudent to describe the test results as being Inconclusive?" he queried.

"Absolutely not," I responded.

When I had entered the office, I wasn't asked to sit down. As the conversation started, both the chief and the case officer rose and stood in front of me. They kept inching forward until they were invading my personal space. Being a typical American who feels uncomfortable when strangers get very close, I kept inching back. I soon found my back against the wall with the two gentlemen close in front of me. Like two lions coming in for the kill, circling and searching for weakness, they increased the verbal pressure. They did their best to break down my confidence level. They asked me about my knowledge of the case, the information made available to me before the test, the clarity of charts obtained, and the level of the agent's English comprehension. They asked me about the possibility of other concerns weighing on the agent's mind that could interfere with the test results. They asked me whether the agent had any health concerns that might have interfered with the test. They both kept on and on with every line of questioning they could think of, all the time suggesting that the test results were really Inconclusive, not Deception Indicated.

The chief asked, "Are you aware of the concerns Headquarters has about the authenticity of the agent?"

"I am," I answered.

He continued, "Do you realize that DI results on a polygraph test would be exactly what Headquarters would need to put an end to our association with the agent?"

"No. I didn't know that, and I'm not sure that's true," I replied.

They continued their onslaught of probing questions and verbal pressure for quite a while, but I didn't waver. I may have been of lower rank than the chief, but I sure knew more about the polygraph process and polygraph professional ethics than those two did. I held my ground, stood firm, and didn't waver from the final DI call I had originally issued. They finally gave up and let me leave the room. Knowing that the chief's position gave him the authority to approve or deny the release of messages to Headquarters, I was relieved to see that my report was eventually released as I had written it. All in all, that was not a pleasant experience.

There was one other occasion when I was pressured, again from the chief of an office. I was within minutes of leaving the office to test an agent who was going to be involved in a diplomatically sensitive and expensive operation.

As I prepared for the case in a vacant office, the chief entered and slowly approached. Putting his knuckles on the desk, he leaned over me, made sure he had my eye, and said, "I expect DI or NDI results."

His words were delivered with all the menace, threat, and intimidation he could muster.

He paused and then added, "I don't want to hear any of that Inconclusive crap."

At first I thought he was joking. His menacing words were delivered in an overbearing, intimidating manner and brought an instant smile to my face, but I quickly saw from the expression on his face that he was dead serious.

As my smile faded, I said, "Sir, I'll do my best to get clear test results, but unfortunately the outcome of some polygraph tests is an Inconclusive call. Sometimes there are health reasons, and sometimes there are just inconsistent and erratic responses for unknown reasons. Inconclusive means you don't know one way or the other. I'm not about to flip a coin just to make it DI or NDI."

"I want DI or NDI," he said, glaring down at me. "That Inconclusive call won't do me any good. We've got an expensive operation about to start, and I've got to know one way or the other."

I repeated, "I'll do my best, but an Inconclusive call is a possibility."

Still hovering over me, he slowly and emphatically repeated, "I want a DI or NDI call." He raised himself to full height again, turned his back to me, and walked out of the office.

Oh, the joys of being the center of attention.

As it turned out, the agent's examination resulted in a clear No Deception Indicated call. The chief's attempts to bully me were totally unnecessary.

Pressure to arrive at a particular decision is not the only kind of outside influence that may influence an examiner's handling of a polygraph case. Fatigue, as experienced with frequent world travel, can also influence examiner's decisions. Illness is another. Competence, or the lack thereof, may be another factor. Today, quality control is an important and integral part of federal polygraph programs. At the CIA, every polygraph examination conducted at Headquarters is reviewed by a polygraph officer serving as an independent, impartial reviewer of the work performed by examiners. The officers serving in this capacity have the authority to overturn the decision made by examiners and direct that the examination continue or that the examinee be scheduled for additional testing. Polygraph cases conducted in the field are also subjected to a quality control review process. In addition to the quality control process performed on every case conducted, quality assurance reviews of completed cases are performed on a random basis, which look at every aspect of a polygraph examination from the interview's beginning to the final report written by the examiner. The polygraph charts are analyzed. A complete review of audio and video recordings of the case is performed, and all the test questions and test formats utilized are studied.

Throughout the 1970s, the office's quality control process was far less stringent. An independent, impartial review of an examiner's work was available, but it primarily existed to assist new examiners. Seasoned examiners in need of a second opinion could also request an independent, impartial review of their case. CIA polygraph training endeavored to produce examiners who were thorough, self-reliant, and confident. Soon after training, examiners handled their polygraph cases independent of supervisory guidance and monitoring, although such assistance was available whenever needed. It was an awesome responsibility to make final polygraph decisions that could potentially impact the lives of the examinees and/or the security of our country. Experienced examiners took that responsibility very seriously. Unfortunately, as in every profession, the polygraph program was not comprised entirely of excellent examiners.

A more formalized quality control program was implemented in the late 1970s guarding against careless work and correcting decisions influenced by fatigue, illness, or political pressure. It proved to be a valuable and necessary element of the polygraph program.

Not long after the quality control program's implementation, entire generations of new examiners were raised in an environment of mandatory quality control reviews of their work. Unlike my early years as a polygraph examiner, examiners were closely monitored, and their work was closely checked by supervisors who served as their quality control officers. Every chart obtained by an examiner was initialed by the supervisor. The supervisor guided and controlled the case. If the supervisor did not agree with the examiner's decision or strategy, the examiner was instructed to interrogate, to continue testing, or to reschedule the examinee for another session.

Alas, as sure as there is good and evil, black and white, and sweet and sour, it seems that along with all good comes some bad. Although the quality control program was undeniably beneficial to the quality of the Section's work, a little bit of bad rode its coattails. I believe my unique position in the office as head of the covert operations polygraph program brought these deleterious effects to my attention, although they went unnoticed by my fellow supervisors working in other polygraph programs.

Polygraph examiners conducted applicant and industrial polygraph cases at Headquarters for more than a year before being introduced to the world of covert ops polygraph. Their initiation to covert ops polygraph began by accompanying a more experienced examiner as he conducted a covert case. Those cases were typically conducted in hotel rooms or safe houses in the Washington DC area. The covert ops trainee would observe the experienced operations examiner handle the case from beginning to end. The experienced examiner would then monitor the trainee as he conducted the second case. The trainee would then conduct his third case unassisted. It was the conduct of such a third case by a young examiner that started me to question the effects of the office's quality control procedures. The examiner was a rising star in the office. He had several years of experience with other types of cases and was considered to be a sharp, by-the-book examiner. He was a master interrogator and an ambitious young officer. I was astonished when I received a telephone call from him while he was at a safe house with a case officer and agent. The conversation went something like this (I'll call the examiner "John"):

ALAN: *Hello.*

JOHN: *Alan? This is John. I'd like your help. I have the case officer and agent in the next room. The case officer is waiting for my final decision. I've finished testing but would like your opinion of the charts.*

ALAN: *What? What's the problem?*

JOHN: *Well, not much really. I'd just like your opinion. I have some responses. Well, I'm not sure they're large enough to call responses. I have some changes I'd like you to weigh in on. You know, before I make the final call.*

ALAN: *I don't quite understand. Are your charts of such poor
quality that you can't make a decision?*

JOHN: *No, not really. I'd just feel more comfortable with your
opinion.*

ALAN: *Are your charts erratic or unreadable?*

JOHN: *No, not at all. I was just hoping I could describe the charts
to you over the telephone.*

ALAN: *How's that? What? What is it you want to do?*

JOHN: *Alan, I thought I could just scan down each chart and
describe to you the changes I see in the tracings for each
parameter.*

ALAN: *What? Are you serious?*

JOHN: *Well, I thought if I did that, you could let me know
whether my analysis is right.*

ALAN: *Look, John. I can't do what you're asking. Just go back
to the case officer and tell him that there are some irreg-
ularities in the agent's charts that you want to bring to
the attention of a quality control officer before you ren-
der a final decision.*

JOHN: *Well, okay, but I told him I'd advise him after I analyzed the charts.*

ALAN: *John, what do you think the final call should be?*

JOHN: *Well, I think it is No Deception Indicated, but I'd like
you to look at my charts.*

ALAN: *John, tell the case officer that you feel no additional testing is necessary and that you'll get the final decision to
him this afternoon.*

JOHN: *Can I describe my charts to you as I scan down each parameter?*

ALAN: *No. You cannot. Come see me as soon as you return to the office.*

JOHN: *Okay.*

Later that day, John presented his examination to me for a quality control review. He advised that his final call was No Deception Indicated. I reviewed his polygraph charts and concurred with his decision. In my debriefing of John, it was obvious to me that he simply felt ill at ease making the final decision on his own, away from the instantaneous supervisory guidance he had been receiving on a daily basis for years. He was certainly a competent and capable examiner, but he found himself in a situation where he was uncomfortable shouldering the responsibility of making polygraph decisions on his own. Now, to be fair to John, I should note that he went on to become an extremely successful, high-ranking polygraph examiner who flourished in the world of covert operations polygraph testing. His biggest cases involved the uncovering of agents who had successfully worked against the CIA for years—until they were polygraphed and interrogated by John.

Unfortunately, John's lack of confidence in making decisions without supervisory guidance was not an isolated incident. After another examiner's first solo case in the Washington DC area, he returned to Headquarters and sought my guidance before providing the case officer with a final call. I reviewed the examiner's charts and completely agreed with his analysis. Once again, there was absolutely no reason for the delay in providing the case officer with a final call. His analysis was flawless, but he lacked self-confidence and felt ill at ease without the support of a hovering supervisor.

After several such experiences, I couldn't help but feel that the stringent quality control program was responsible for promoting a lack of confidence and slowing the development of independence in new examiners. At the very least, I believed the quality control program was delaying the development of these characteristics that were so important in a field examiner.

One day, trying to solidify some of my growing suspicions about the effects of the office's quality control program, I engaged an examiner in conversation. I must admit, I had little expectation of getting truthful replies to any questions I might pose about our office's quality control methods. I guided our conversation to such topics as people in the office, caseloads, and particular supervisors, until I finally talked about supervisors guiding examiners and reviewing their work.

I stated, "You know, in my early years, supervisors did not check my polygraph charts and review the final calls I made. It must be a very comfortable feeling to know that your supervisors also take some responsibility if you make bad decisions."

With unexpected frankness and candor, the examiner replied, "You bet! As far as I am concerned, he takes full responsibility. His initials are on every polygraph chart. His name is on record as the reviewing officer and the one who released both the findings and the polygraph report to the adjudicators. He has a higher grade and is in a supervisory position. No question about it. The responsibility is his."

After some additional analysis, I came to realize that some examiners were mere puppets on a string who danced to the tune of their supervisor. They were polygraph operators, not polygraph examiners, and would never do well in the role of a field examiner. They flourished under the control and direction of a supervisor. On the other hand, there were other examiners who were naturally self-confident and independent. I also realized that there were supervisors who strove to develop examiners to be self-reliant and confident, but there also were others who felt as long as their name was associated with a case, they were going to make sure that no mistakes were made. They guided, commanded, and directed their examiners to the point of making the final call for them. Some examiners did not mind this arrangement.

As head of the covert ops polygraph program, I helped examiners overcome their reliance on the rigid quality control system when they were introduced to operational cases. With the help of senior examiners, it took time to wean some examiners from this kind of relationship when they started conducting cases away from the Headquarters environment. However, I was pleased that virtually all thrived in their newfound independence.

Chapter Fifteen

The John Wayne Impersonator

Always tell the truth. If you can't tell the truth, don't lie.

—AUTHOR UNKNOWN

Most polygraph examiners have an excellent sense of humor, although some of their friends might describe it as being dark or sick at times. In my opinion, the sense of humor developed by many examiners is a coping mechanism designed to help them live with all the despicable information they routinely encounter on the job. Other professionals who deal with human tragedy and depravity also develop a comparable dark sense of humor. Professionals that immediately come to mind are police, psychologists, doctors, nurses, and paramedics.

I have found a sense of humor to be absolutely necessary to survive as a polygraph examiner and interrogator. Although the vast majority of polygraph subjects I tested were decent people who just wanted a security clearance and a job with the CIA, I encountered decent people who occasionally did bad, disgusting things. On the other hand, I encountered others who were not good people and should not work for the CIA or have top secret security clearances. As an examiner and interrogator, I may have been personally disgusted and repulsed by the behavior of a subject, but I could never display my true feelings. People don't feel comfortable confiding in someone who expresses disgust, contempt, or disapproval of their behavior. I could not be judgmental while listening to accounts of their misdeeds. I avoided berating or chastising a subject, and I never expressed moral indignation. Instead, in order to elicit all the grisly details of people's nasty, evil deeds, I empathized, sympathized, and provided excuses to make it easier for them to rationalize their behavior. I made it easier for the subject to reveal, rather than to conceal, the information being withheld. I, as well as my colleagues, found it to be an emotionally taxing job at times when dealing with vile people who have done illegal, perverted, evil deeds.

Because of the nature and demands of the work, some wannabe examiners never make it through basic training. Some realize at some point during training, or soon after training, that they do not have the mental fortitude for this kind of work. Some examiners might survive a year or more on the job before they recognize how unhappy or ill the job has made them and move on to other kinds of work, as well they should.

Those who persevere in this profession seem to develop a rather healthy sense of humor as a coping mechanism. The more creative ones gravitate toward playing practical jokes on each other. This activity sometimes begins early in their careers by sabotaging each other's polygraph equipment just for the pleasure of placing their fellow examiners in uncomfortable positions as they try to conduct professional interviews. For example, rubber tubing on an examiner's equipment would be connected to the wrong ports, good batteries would be exchanged with dead ones, or messages and pictures would be pasted on chart paper (noticeable only after ten feet of paper had rolled out to ensure the examiner would be in the midst of collecting test data when he discovered the picture). Quick-drying ink would be substituted for regular polygraph ink so that pens would rapidly clog. Phony polygraph case files containing bogus information would be given to an unsuspecting examiner who thought he was assigned a legitimate case. The savvy examiners usually caught the tampering before much damage was done to an ongoing polygraph case, but the more gullible ones were usually caught off guard, and therefore targeted more often.

Practical jokes between CIA examiners were by no means confined to the United States. An infamous series of practical jokes played on one examiner may have actually been responsible for a change in his career path. The examiner was slated to fill a polygraph officer PCS position in Southeast Asia. Prior to taking the new assignment, he had been selected to TDY to that location to assist two other examiners already there on TDY with a heavy caseload. The TDY was viewed by Polygraph Section management as an excellent opportunity for him to have an orientation trip to the country where he was going to spend the next two or three years of his life.

After the examiner had worked in the country for several days during the TDY, he made the deadly mistake of revealing personal information to the other two examiners over drinks in the evening. He told them he arrived at his hotel after work the previous evening feeling rather tense and exhausted. The grueling airplane trip from the United States, coupled with the heavy schedule of cases at the office and the change in time zones, had taken its toll. He noticed that his hotel had hot bath and massage service, so he made an appointment for himself. He told the examiners what a wonderfully refreshing and relaxing experience it had been. The examiner's openness was his undoing, because he forgot for a moment that he was talking with two highly skilled interrogators. Both had the reputation for being able to talk a snake into paying in advance for a year's worth of tap dancing lessons. Also, both had a penchant for playing practical jokes on their fellow examiners. With all the tenacity and perseverance the two examiners were famous for, they launched into an interrogation of the examiner on the "massage story." They were so adept at performing subtle interrogations that the examiner may have never even realized he was being interrogated. They managed to convince him that the massage service in his hotel was actually one of the city's most notorious locations where customers received "special" massages. They tried many subtle elicitation and interrogation techniques to extract an admission of receiving a "special" massage. They persisted, the examiner resisted, and then they eventually desisted. Unbeknownst to the examiner, their goal that evening was not to get an admission of wrongdoing. They were merely setting groundwork.

Several days later, wanting to spend a quiet evening in his hotel room, the examiner did not join the other two for drinks and dinner after work. His absence gave the two an opportunity to mount a wicked practical joke. They engaged the services of a local hostess who spoke English well enough to help them with their prank. They took some time explaining the scenario to her and coached her on what to say in the role they asked her to play in their ruse. Then, as they stood next to her, they had the hostess call the examiner's hotel room. The conversation went something like this:

EXAMINER: *Hello.*

HOSTESS: *Good evening, sir. This is Somsri at the front desk.*

EXAMINER: *Yes?*

HOSTESS: *Sir, I am sorry to disturb you, but there is a problem with your bill.*

EXAMINER: *Problem? What problem?*

HOSTESS: *Sir, you had a massage at the hotel two days ago?*

EXAMINER: *Yes, I did.*

HOSTESS: *Sir, you didn't pay the entire bill.*

EXAMINER: *Wait a minute. I paid the bill in full.*

HOSTESS: *Sir, there was a $20 charge on the bill. I guess you forgot to pay it.*

EXAMINER: *What? Charge for what?*

HOSTESS: *Sir, you got a massage? That is correct?*

EXAMINER: *Yes, I did. That is correct.*

HOSTESS: *Sir, there was a $20 charge for the special.*

EXAMINER: *What?*

HOSTESS: *Sir, you didn't pay the $20. You know, for the special.*

EXAMINER: *Special? I didn't get any special.*

HOSTESS: *Sir, the bill clearly has the charges listed for the bath, the massage, and the special. You only paid for the bath and the massage.*

EXAMINER: *I only had a bath and a massage. I didn't get any special.*

HOSTESS: *Sir, it's not nice to ask the young lady for the special and not pay for it.*

EXAMINER: *I didn't ask for and I didn't get a special.*

HOSTESS: *Sir, you must be a very bad man.*

EXAMINER: *Look, I'm coming right down to straighten this out. What's your name again?*

HOSTESS: *Somsri.*

EXAMINER: *I'll be down in a minute.*

They both hung up. I'm sure that the two examiners grinned broadly. Perhaps, they even fell down on the floor in fits of uncontrollable hoots and snorts over the success of their ruse. I can only imagine the confusing scene at the front desk at his hotel as the examiner stormed down to confront Somsri over the $20 charge for the "special" on his bill. As I understand it, the examiner never spoke of the incident with the other two examiners.

Unfortunately for the examiner, the story does not end there. His colleagues had one more practical joke concocted for his last day in country. They knew that his flight on Pan Am was departing the international airport early the next morning at 8:00 A.M. The examiner had complained about how early the flight was and how difficult it was going to be to wake up early to take the hour-long taxi ride and arrive at the airport one hour before departure. Providing information like that to those two was like giving them the keys to your house.

Once again, the two engaged the services of a local hostess who spoke some English, and once again they explained the scenario to her and coached her on what to say in the role they asked her to take in their new hoax. That evening they had her call the examiner's hotel room. The conversation went something like this:

EXAMINER: *Hello.*

HOSTESS: *Good evening, sir. This is Kongchu. I am a representative in the reservations department at Pan Am. How are you tonight?*

EXAMINER: *Fine.*

HOSTESS: *I am so glad I got in touch with you tonight. I am trying to get in touch with all our passengers leaving tomorrow morning.*

EXAMINER: *Yes?*

HOSTESS: *Sir, there has been a change in your departure time tomorrow.*

EXAMINER: *What!*

HOSTESS: *Yes. You are on the flight leaving at eight A.M. Right?*

EXAMINER: *That's right.*

HOSTESS: *That flight will now depart at six A.M.*

EXAMINER: *Six A.M.? Why?*

HOSTESS: *There has been a change in the plane's routing, so it must now depart at six A.M.*

EXAMINER: *Well, okay.*

HOSTESS: *Sir, there is one more thing.*

EXAMINER: *Yes.*

HOSTESS: *With the new security checks we have had to put in place before boarding, you should be at the airport two hours early.*

EXAMINER: *At four A.M.?*

HOSTESS: *Yes, sir.*

The spirited pair of mischief makers struck again. The examiner left his hotel at 3:00 A.M. to arrive at the international airport at 4:00 A.M. for an 8:00 A.M. departure. Shortly after his return to the United States, the examiner advised Polygraph Section management that he wanted to decline the overseas PCS assignment for personal reasons.

I have always wondered whether those practical jokes had anything to do with his decision.

I was almost the target of one of their pranks on several occasions. I narrowly escaped. As it turned out, I didn't need their help to be put in a foolish situation. My own guarded nature, along with an expectation of a practical joke coming around the corner when I least expected it, proved to be my undoing during one of my trips to South America. It was a July day, and I found myself in a capital city I had visited a half-dozen times before. The office was medium-sized as CIA offices go. I was alone on the trip and had a number of cases scheduled for several case officers. I conducted one of the cases midday on July 3. The case was routine and unremarkable, and the case officer and I found ourselves returning to the office before the close of business. As we entered the office area, we walked in on their Fourth of July celebration. There were food tables set up with sandwiches, chips, cake, and punch. There were noisy groups of people congregating throughout the area. Since I didn't recognize everyone, I gathered that people outside the office had been invited to join the celebration.

The case officer said, "Alan, drop your gear and please join us."

I didn't have to be asked twice. I got some food, cake, and punch and then found a quiet corner. As I ate, I watched all the people in festive spirits engaged in loud conversations. After a while, the case officer approached me with someone in tow.

"Alan, I'd like to introduce you to someone," he said. "Alan, this is the American ambassador."

My practical joke radar shot up at that moment. *Surely, this man cannot be the ambassador,* I thought. He was scruffy looking, with shoulder-length hair and a beard. He looked young. He looked exactly like someone's son who was home visiting his parents on a summer break from graduate school in the United States. He was the antithesis of my image of an ambassador.

I was absolutely convinced the case officer was trying to pull a practical joke on me, so in a sarcastic tone I replied, "Yeah, right. I'm John Wayne. It's nice to meet the head honcho—a man with sand, no doubt."

If the "ambassador" could pretend to be someone he was not, so could I. I intended to show the case officer that he was not clever enough to fool me.

The gentleman tried to engage me in some conversation. He asked about my work at the office and what brought me to the country. I kept playing the game and delivered another smart-aleck answer.

"Bringing the pilgrims across the mountains by wagon train was tough. I had to kill a few Indians, but they had it coming. Anyway, the only good Indian is a dead Indian. Right? After all, a man's got to do what a man's got to do," I said.

Trying to quote John Wayne, I added, "After all, I won't be wronged, I won't be insulted, and I won't be laid a hand on. I don't do these things to other people and I expect the same from them."

He eyed me strangely, tried to ask me a few more questions, and then moved on to talk with someone else. I find it hard to blame him. If I was an ambassador and found myself talking to a deranged man with a mind like mine, I would move on, too. And yes, he really was the ambassador.

Chapter Sixteen

The Perilous World of Espionage

There is nothing so powerful as truth—and often nothing so strange.

—DANIEL WEBSTER

Espionage is a violation of both U.S. law (Title 18, Chapter 37, Sections 792–799 of U.S. Code) and the Uniform Code of Military Justice (Article 106). It is defined by the Department of Defense as, "The act of obtaining, delivering, transmitting, communicating, or receiving information about the national defense with an intent, or reason to believe, that the information may be used to the injury of the United States or to the advantage of any foreign nation." Since foreign governments have similar laws, the conduct of a polygraph

examination on foreign soil puts the case officer, polygraph examiner, and agent in a precarious position if captured in an act of espionage. The risks are great and the
penalties can be high if apprehended. Arrest, deportation,
imprisonment, and execution are all possible outcomes.
More often than not, foreigners caught in the act of espionage have been declared Personae Non Grata and were
expelled from the country. The host country's citizen caught
with the foreigners received the harshest punishment.

The United States, as well as most other foreign governments, conducts espionage against other countries. It
matters not whether other countries are allies or foes. Acts
of espionage have occurred between countries throughout
history. Interestingly, it is modern literature and cinema that
have popularized the activity, the players, and the organizations that conduct espionage on behalf of their governments. The activities of the CIA, the KGB, Jack Ryan, Jason
Bourne, and James Bond are familiar to people all over the
world.

It is the arrival of the newest players in the spy game,
organizations involved in the trafficking of illegal drugs and
those involved in international terrorism, that has changed
the playing field. Narco-traffickers and terrorists have their
own intelligence apparatus to protect their activities and
counter those who oppose them. It has been my experience
that narco-traffickers and terrorists are not very nice people, as evidenced by the estimated 120,000 deaths in the
Mexico Drug War and 3,000 deaths from the September 11,
2001 attacks. They do not worry about the sensitive nature

of politics between countries. They do not declare people Personae Non Grata; they terminate people. The risk of receiving the harshest of penalties if caught increased with the addition of the new players in the game.

When I conducted tests and interrogations in support of a counternarcotics program, there was no longer a concern of being apprehended by the host government for espionage activities. In fact, the host government knew who I was, and they knew what I did. They even knew what hotel I stayed at during my visit. Although this might sound like a relaxing break for a polygraph examiner who is normally concerned about conducting his business in a clandestine manner, this type of polygraph examination brought a new set of concerns.

Examinations were conducted on the new recruits of counternarcotics programs. The tests administered were very narrow in scope, with the key issue covering whether the examinee was on the payroll of the narco-traffickers. Unfortunately, that was not an uncommon situation. When a soldier or police officer received an offer that was the equivalent to one year's salary to simply look the other way when a truck passed through a checkpoint, they often found it difficult to refuse the offer. My concern while working on such programs was that I was openly identified to the program's leaders. They knew where I slept at night, and I knew that counternarcotics programs were frequently infiltrated. Without a doubt, I would certainly be perceived as a threat if I exposed penetrations of the counternarcotics program. When walking out of my hotel each morning, there was always the lingering apprehension of being strafed by machine gun fire from a passing vehicle. When I went to sleep each night, there was always the thought that the entire hotel could be burned to the ground while I slept, just to eliminate me. However, other than learning that examinees I previously tested had lost their lives in the drug war, all my cases were safely accomplished.

It mattered not whether I performed polygraph tests and interrogations in support of counterintelligence, narcotics, or terrorist programs. My participation in all of them was a perilous undertaking. Actually, the vast majority of the operational polygraph work I performed overseas was in direct support of the National Clandestine Service's program to validate its assets. I conducted the cases in a clandestine fashion and utilized appropriate tradecraft to ensure that the meetings went undetected by the local police, security, or intelligence services. My true identity was always withheld from the agents, and my cover was always designed to conceal my true employer from host government officials. Because my polygraph exploits overseas were frequent and numerous, I am reasonably certain that many foreign governments strongly suspected (perhaps even knew for sure) that I was a polygraph examiner for an American intelligence service.

Although every examination was a potentially dangerous undertaking, my capture and arrest was never so close as on a case I once conducted in the capital city of a South American country. The agent was a prolific producer of information on activities within the government, although he was not a member of any host government security or intelligence service. Perhaps, I should say he was not known by the case officer to have any such position.

His polygraph examination was considered to be routine. It was requested by the office as part of their attempt to validate their stable of agents. After reviewing the agent's file and discussing the case with the case officer, I had every expectation of conducting a routine examination that would be accomplished in a two- or three-hour time frame.

An old Polygraph Section adage states that what appears to be the nastiest, most complicated case with the thickest file, full of suspicions and allegations often turns out to be the easiest case to conduct. On the other hand, the case that appears to be simple, straightforward, and routine may turn out to be the one that requires a lengthy interrogation leading to significant confessions and a lengthy polygraph report. The case I handled on that trip supported the adage's contentions.

Most covert cases were handled overseas in a professional, secure, and clandestine fashion. This case was no exception. The safe house chosen for its conduct was an apartment that had all the furnishings I needed to conduct a comfortable, professional interview. The case officer escorted me to the site first and then left me there while he met the agent elsewhere in the city. After retrieving the agent, he escorted him to the safe house. I was introduced to the agent as Mr. Johnson, a name I selected to use during many of my operational cases.

There were no outward indications that the examination was anything but another routine test. The agent seemed to have an entirely appropriate and acceptable amount of general nervous tension. His behavior was not out of the ordinary in any way. He listened attentively and fully cooperated with my test instructions. He had the normal amount of concern and asked typical questions about the polygraph process.

All of the test questions were reviewed and thoroughly discussed with the agent prior to conducting the tests. The agent fully understood each question and assured me that he was able to provide completely confident and truthful answers to each of the questions. Up to that point in the polygraph interview, everything had transpired exactly as I had expected. I felt that the process of collecting polygraph charts was simply going to substantiate that the agent had indeed provided confident and truthful answers to the test questions and that we would all soon be finished with the interview and move on with the rest of our day.

When I conducted a series of polygraph tests on the questions, an unfortunate and unexpected end was put to the routine nature of the interview. A student in polygraph training would have been able to clearly analyze the charts I had collected. All test questions had been asked several times during several separate tests, and the agent produced consistent, unmistakable reactions to two key questions. Despite his claims during our pretest discussion, the agent had not provided confident and truthful answers. His answers were clearly deceptive. The case officer, Chris, waiting in an adjoining room, was probably anxious to get a status report on the results of testing, but I decided to query the agent for a moment to gauge his mental fortitude.

"Thank you for your cooperation," I said. "The quality of your test is very good. I will be able to easily analyze your charts. Before I do a thorough and final analysis, can you tell me whether you felt ill at ease with your answer to any particular question on the test? Did any one of the question make you feel more uncomfortable than the others?"

"All the questions were the same. I was not ill at ease with any one of them," he replied.

"Okay. It will help me to analyze your test results if I know what you were thinking during the test. What were your thoughts or concerns?" I asked.

"I remembered hearing that the polygraph instrument is not accurate," he answered.

"Look," I said. "Let's say there were two shooters at the firing range. One shooter picked up a rifle, aimed at the target down range, and put six consecutive shots in the bull's-eye. The second shooter then picked up the same rifle and only put three of his six shots in the bull's-eye. Was that rifle one hundred percent accurate or fifty percent accurate? I think you can see that the rifle's accuracy depended on the training and skill of the shooter. Well, like that rifle, the polygraph instrument is a calibrated, precision instrument that does exactly what it was designed to do. More importantly, the CIA has the most highly trained and skilled polygraph examiners in the world. Now, let's set that concern aside. What other thoughts or concerns did you have?"

"I had no other thoughts or concerns," he answered.

"Tell me about any issues you have on these questions," I said.

"Issues? What kind of issues?" he asked.

"Well, let's see. For example, it is not uncommon for people to apply past experiences from their life to the topics covered by these test questions. Everyone has life experiences. I have mine. You have yours. These questions cause me to reflect on experiences I've had. What experiences from your past do you apply to these questions?" I queried.

"None," he replied.

It was easy to tell from his answers that he was responding in a guarded fashion. He was carefully choosing his words and offering very little regarding thought processes that anyone would have in similar circumstances. During pretest discussion, he gave every appearance of being forthcoming and cooperative, but his behavior had now changed.

"All right," I continued. "But you know what I think? I think you are a very intelligent man. If you were an uneducated dolt sitting in that chair, I could understand how you would have no thoughts. If you suffered brain damage after an accident, I could understand how you would have no thoughts. But you are a very intelligent man. I've been doing this work for many years, and I know as well as anyone that intelligent people's brains are constantly thinking. When an intelligent person hears a test question, he answers the question, but then his mind reflects in some manner on the topic of the question. If you were not reflecting on your own life experiences, who else were you thinking about during the test?"

"No one," he replied.

"Which friend or business associate did you think about?" I asked.

"No friend. No business associate," he emphatically replied.

"What family member?" I asked.

"No family member," was his simple response.

"Is there any reason, any reason that we have not discussed, that would cause you to react to any of these test questions?" I queried.

"No," he replied in his recently adopted manner of warily providing guarded answers. I also noted a hint of suspicion entering his demeanor. I explained that I needed to perform a final analysis of his tests and that I would retire to the adjoining room for a few minutes.

In the adjoining room, I briefed Chris on the status of the polygraph interview. I explained that the agent had clearly reacted to a question that dealt with revealing his secret relationship with American intelligence to unauthorized people, as well as to another about having a secret relationship with another intelligence service. I told him of the agent's responses to my initial probing questions and explained that the next step would be to confront him with the test results and begin an interrogation in an attempt to extract the truth. Chris wanted me to proceed. The agent was a prolific producer of information and a valuable asset for the office. Chris wanted to salvage the situation if it was at all possible. Both of us felt that salvaging the situation would undoubtedly be difficult if the session were to end with deceptive polygraph test results accompanied by no explanations from the agent.

I have heard stories from other polygraph examiners about overseas covert ops interrogations that lasted for three or four days. Stories of those interrogations were told, not necessarily because of the length of the interrogation, but because of the examiners' success in obtaining admissions from an agent about working against the Agency for many years. After all, catching a spy working against the CIA is the ultimate success story for a polygraph examiner.

Most routine polygraph examinations of agents overseas lasted approximately two to four hours. The difficult ones, the ones that involved interrogation and additional testing, lasted approximately six to eight hours. My case involved two days of interrogation and testing.

When I continued the agent's polygraph interview, I confronted him with the results of his tests and launched into an interrogation. The interrogation was lengthy, and I am sure that I used every tool in my interrogation tool bag. It was long, arduous work on my part. I could see the agent was conflicted, unsure of his next course of action.

After the dinner hour had come and gone, I realized we had been involved in a match of wits for about ten hours and needed something substantial to eat. The case officer and the agent left the safe house to search for a local restaurant, and I headed in the opposite direction to find another place to dine.

I immediately detected a change in the agent's demeanor when I continued with the interrogation back in the safe house after dinner. He seemed defeated, as if he had reconsidered his position during the break. I still detected evidence of mental anguish, but he seemed to be ready to tell me something significant regarding the issues of concern. Not long after I noticed the changes in his behavior, he confessed.

The agent stated that soon after he agreed to enter into a secret relationship with American intelligence, he sought out a similar relationship with the intelligence service of a neighboring country. Greed was his motivation, fueled by receiving a regular paycheck from us for providing information. For him, the work was easy and the pay was good. He reasoned he could provide the same information to another service and get paid twice for working once.

The agent's confession was certainly significant. It was directly related to the questions he had reacted to during testing, and it involved information that he desired to keep secret from the case officer. The confession was plausible. I had obtained similar confessions during other agent cases. Greed is a universal sin that apparently knows no boundaries.

I briefed the case officer. He was surprised but was quick to add that the situation was not a deal breaker. It was obvious he wanted to continue the relationship. I explained that additional polygraph testing was needed to verify that the agent had revealed the full extent of his concerns. Due to the lateness of the hour, we decided to terminate the interview for the day and to continue the session the next day.

I spent quite a while with the agent to make sure he left with his ego intact. I prepared him for the continuation of the session and explained what we expected to accomplish during the next day's meeting. The officer left with the agent to see him safely out, and I stayed in the safe house to pack up the polygraph equipment while awaiting his return. While he was gone, I replayed the many hours of interrogation in my mind. A feeling of dissatisfaction slowly set in. There were still many unanswered questions. Why had the agent resisted for so long? Although significant, his confession was not that damaging to the ongoing relationship he had with us. It didn't make sense to me. The two issues he strongly reacted to involved revealing his secret relationship with us to unauthorized persons and having a secret relationship with another intelligence service. To whom had he revealed the secret relationship? Did he have a secret relationship with any intelligence service besides the one he mentioned? Did he have a secret relationship with any host government intelligence service? Had he been directed against us by any intelligence service? Was he reporting to anyone on his contacts with the case officer? Despite a confession of seeming significance, the unanswered questions left me with the knowledge that the case was far from being resolved. Did I truly have a whole confession, or did I have the tip of an iceberg?

All interrogation officers are familiar with a concept called "throwing a bone," wherein an examinee offers an interrogator information to throw him off track. It is a stalling tactic, usually an act of desperation, used in the hope that the interrogator will take that bone and run with it for a while and perhaps even believe that the bone is the truth, the whole truth, and nothing but the truth. A "bone" may be information fabricated by the agent, it may be a partial truth, and it may be an entirely true piece of information, but it most certainly is not the information that the examinee was really concealing during interrogation. After a lengthy interrogation, a confession will many times be treated by an interrogator as a bone thrown by the examinee. The interrogator will say something like, "John, thanks for telling me that, but that could not possibly explain the massive reactions I saw on your polygraph charts. Something much more serious than that caused you to react. John, what else is there?" The interrogator will continue with the interrogation as if there had been no confession. If what the examinee said was truly the reason for his reactions, he will continue to offer his story over and over again, because he has nothing else to add.

The more I thought about the interrogation I had conducted and the plausibility of the confession I had obtained, the more I thought it was a bone the examinee had decided to offer. I made up my mind to treat the confession as a bone when I continued with the interview the next day. By the time I turned out the light that night, I was convinced that I didn't have the whole truth.

We regrouped at the safe house the following morning. I was a little surprised that the agent followed through with his agreement to meet with the case officer. After surviving his day-long polygraph session, I expected him to have little incentive to continue. He must have been convinced that the case officer and I believed his admission was the reason for his test reactions. He must have been desperate to have his working relationship with us continue.

I began the second day of the agent's polygraph interview as if there had been no explanation or confession the day before. He attempted to proffer his story once again, but I quickly dismissed it as I would dismiss any other suspected bone. He didn't try to offer his explanation again during hours of subsequent interrogation. Of course, that gave credence to my belief that his confession had in fact been a bone thrown my way.

The second day proved to be as arduous as the first, for both of us, I am sure. We all broke for lunch and then continued into the afternoon. I was repetitive, tenacious, and persistent; but the agent countered my advance with his stubbornness and resistance. His resolve was unyielding. By midafternoon, I decided to conduct additional polygraph testing to use as a guide for further interrogation. I needed to focus more on the agent's area of concern, but I wasn't sure whether that involved working for a yet to be revealed intelligence service, reporting to a host government intelligence service, reporting on his contacts with his case officer, or being directed against American intelligence.

The results of the additional testing clearly indicated

that the agent worked for a host government intelligence service and had been directed against us. Following the test, but before confronting the agent any further, I briefed Chris on the results. He was both astounded and confused. We tried to ascertain what the opposition would gain from the arrangement. Was it to provide us with disinformation? Was it to obtain information on Chris? Were they interested in his requirements, modus operandi, or the training of and means of communication with the agent?

The interrogation of the agent continued throughout the afternoon, but I was unable to obtain any new information. The session was terminated at the end of the day. The agent was strong willed and unbending in his denials. I failed to convince him that it was in his best interest to reveal the truth, probably because he clearly realized it was not. He evidently understood that denial was his best course of action, and I was unable to change his mind. On the other hand, the polygraph evidence was crystal clear. From my analysis of the test questions asked, there was simply no doubt that the agent was working for or reporting to a host government intelligence service and that he had been directed to work against us.

That was the last case on my schedule for that visit to the city. The next day, I discussed the case with both the case officer and the chief of the office and then prepared my report of the lengthy, two-day session. Unfortunately, my work continued on into the evening, since I also had to finalize reports from other polygraph sessions conducted earlier. Chris graciously offered to stay with me in order to lock up the office when I finished my work. When my work was completed, it was dark outside, and we both left the building together. Chris headed in one direction for his car in the parking lot, and I headed for the main thoroughfare to walk the several blocks to my hotel.

It was a very pleasant evening and it felt good to stretch my legs. My hotel was located on a side street off the main thoroughfare. As I approached within one hundred feet of the entrance, I spied a car on my side of the street, parked at the curb and pointed in my direction. I noticed two men sitting in the front seat, both appearing to watch my approach with fixated stares. As I neared the car, I recognized the driver. He was the agent I had just interrogated for the past two days in the safe house. He smiled, pointed an index finger at me and twitched his thumb down as if firing a pretend pistol, just like children do when they play cops and robbers. His passenger performed the same pretend pistol firing maneuver. Stunned by this surprise encounter, I simply nodded, kept walking, and entered my hotel. As I walked past the car, I initially thought his presence at my hotel must have been purely coincidental. I wondered whether he had been outside the hotel on some kind of business as I happened by. Unfortunately, in the covert activities business of the intelligence world, a coincidence is often nothing more than a well-hidden plot. I was worried.

Alone in my hotel room, I reflected further on the unexpected encounter. I was once again faced with many unanswered questions. Was it a chance encounter or was he waiting for me to return to my hotel? How did he know which hotel I was staying at? Who was the other man with him? What was the meaning of the pretend pistol firing? Why had the other man performed the same maneuver?

It was either a planned or chance encounter, and I could not decide at the time which made more sense. I suspected he either had the authority or the connections to have me arrested if he so desired, but since that did not occur outside the hotel, I thought it unlikely to occur that night. Since I was leaving the country the following morning for the next stop on my swing through South America, I finished packing my suitcase and eventually fell asleep after reading some more of a spy novel that I hoped would relax me, but probably did nothing but fuel my concerns and suspicions.

Upon leaving my hotel the following morning, I felt compelled to glance over to the spot where the agent had been parked the night before. As I had hoped, he wasn't there. I began to feel silly about my suspicions of our encounter. Unquestionably, it had been a strange encounter, but I now thought without a doubt, it must have been a chance encounter.

The taxi ride to the airport and my processing through the check-in counter at the airport were uneventful. I proceeded to the departure lounge and sat down to continue reading the spy novel as I waited for the boarding announcement. The lounge quickly filled with passengers for the flight, and the area became rather noisy, but I immersed myself in my novel and waited. Finally, the boarding announcement was aired over the loudspeaker system in both

English and Spanish, and a line formed. I got in line with
the others and slowly made my way to the airline representative taking boarding passes at the passageway entrance.
I slowly moved forward in line and got within eyesight of
the entrance. I saw the airline representative taking passengers' boarding passes, but I also saw two gentlemen
dressed in business suits sitting in chairs, one on each side
of the entrance. My heart sank and my stomach churned.
The agent was sitting on the right side, and the other man
from the night before was sitting on the left side. They both
glared at me as I approached. Someone once said, "Once
is chance, twice is a coincidence, three times is an enemy
action." I didn't need a third time to realize their presence
was an enemy action. There was no doubt he was there to
make me pay the fiddler for our little dance the day before.

Fear sent a chill down my spine. As I handed my boarding pass to the airline representative, both men stared me
straight in the eye. I thought I caught a wink, but there was
no accompanying smile from either one of them. Once
again they pointed their index fingers at me and brought
their thumbs down mimicking the firing of a pistol. Neither of them made any attempt to prevent me from boarding the aircraft. As I did the night before, I simply nodded
and kept walking.

My mind raced, and I was filled with fear as I took my
seat on the airplane. I fully expected the two of them to
follow me on board to arrest me, and I sat in my seat waiting for my world to come crashing to an end. They never
boarded, and the airplane eventually pulled away from the

terminal, taxied down the runway, and lifted off to speed me away from the nightmarish predicament below.

Thousands of feet aloft in the air, I was finally able to fully relax, actually for the first time since encountering the agent outside my hotel the night before. There was now little doubt that the agent had been working in some fashion for the host government's intelligence service. Also, pretending to shoot me when we faced each other outside the hotel and then again while I boarded the airplane was a menacing gesture designed to tell me that they could have arrested me any time they wanted. I got the message.

I reported the incident to Headquarters after arriving at my next stop, but I never heard what happened to the agent. Considering the deceptive results of his two-day polygraph examination, I assume the case officer terminated their relationship.

I was fortunate that the players in the spy game on that occasion were neither narco-traffickers nor terrorists. Narco-traffickers and terrorists might have played by different rules, perhaps with real guns. Although I presume the agent's government decided the political gain of my arrest was not worth the trouble, my capture and arrest never seemed so close as it was on that occasion. Playing in the game of espionage is certainly a perilous undertaking.

Chapter Seventeen

Security First

It is always the best policy to speak the truth,
unless, of course, you are an exceptionally
good liar.

—JEROME K. JEROME

Since arrest and incarceration were always possible outcomes of covert operations polygraph cases gone bad, I always considered basic common sense to be of paramount importance. Although I strived to handle field examinations efficiently, comfortably, and safely through the use of appropriate tradecraft, it was the application of basic, commonsense measures during field polygraph tests that I felt prevented my arrest. I tried to plan for all contingencies. Unfortunately, the world of covert polygraph tests was fertile ground for unplanned, unexpected events.

On one of my trips to South America I found myself in a coastal city with quite a few cases on my schedule. It was not the capital city, but it was still fairly large, and it had a few large hotels. When a hotel is used for the conduct of a field case, a large hotel is the best choice. It is much easier to keep a low profile. The larger hotels have many people coming in and out of the lobby at all hours, as well as many people using the elevators. When you walk into the lobby of a small hotel, you always feel like all the hotel employees are watching you, because that is usually exactly what they are doing. During my visit, I had successfully completed several cases for the office, with a different hotel used for each case. The case officer selected a small hotel for my final case. After he escorted me to the hotel room, he left to pluck the agent from a nearby street corner. The room was very small, but adequately furnished, and it met my needs for the conduct of the examination. The simplicity of the case and the suitability of the testing site gave me every hope of being able to chalk up another routine case that would be safely conducted without incident. After entering the room, I surveyed its contents and then proceeded to move the furniture around to properly configure it for the polygraph interview.

After the case officer had returned to the hotel room with the agent, I asked, "Did you secure the deadbolt on the door?"

"Sure did," he replied.

As bad luck would have it, I was either lax or forgetful that day, as I failed to follow my own advice to always double-check on security arrangements handled by others. I didn't check the door myself. I had merely asked about the deadbolt.

A significant portion of my life has been spent in hotel rooms. During my stays in hotel rooms, there have been numerous occasions when hotel maids knocked on the door and then immediately barged into the room with a pass-key. Some even just barged in without knocking. So, knowing that this can and does happen, the prudent course of action would be to make sure it doesn't happen during the conduct of a polygraph case of a foreign agent.

During the examination, the agent sat in a chair in the center of the room, next to the coffee table, facing the hotel room door. I sat on the couch beside the coffee table, and the case officer sat on the other side of the agent serving as my interpreter. As the interview was nearing the midway point, I was in the process of collecting a polygraph chart on questions that had been reviewed with the agent when I heard a key being inserted in the door lock. I paused in midsentence and turned toward the door, the agent stopped breathing, and the case officer dropped the set of questions that were in his hands. As the case officer and I glared at the door, both fearing that the local security or intelligence service was barging in, the doorknob jiggled, the door swung wide open, and the maid walked in. She trotted across the room straight toward the three of us and stopped about five feet away, staring wide-eyed and openmouthed at the agent connected to the polygraph instrument. Her eyes followed the rubber tubing and wires that connected the pneumograph tube, GSR, and blood pressure cuff on the agent to the polygraph instrument. Chart paper was still scrolling out and pens were still scratching red ink tracings. The maid was speechless, obviously aghast at the proceedings she had stumbled upon. I think she would have been less surprised if she had stumbled upon two lovers caught in an act of reckless debauchery. The case officer leaped up and angrily told her to leave.

She left, but needless to say, we hastily packed up the polygraph instrument and left the hotel as rapidly as we could. I don't know whether the maid reported her encounter to the hotel manager or to the police, but I do know I had no desire to be questioned by either. We were fortunate that our departure from the hotel went unnoticed.

With sufficient resources and manpower, a determined foreign intelligence service can discover and interfere with a "clandestine" polygraph test. It never left my mind that the agent was the weak link in my attempts to address security and safety issues. After all, without the extra sense of security the administration of a polygraph examination gave, I was never sure whether an operation was secure or compromised. I was never sure whether or not the local security or intelligence service was aware of the agent's relationship with us. Since the weak link is the agent, the question always surfaces, "Should we tell the agent in advance that he's going to be polygraphed?"

There are two schools of thought regarding the notification of an agent of an impending polygraph examination.
The first school believes that the agent should not be told
in advance. When he arrives at what he believes to be a regularly scheduled meeting with his case officer, the agent
should be introduced to the polygraph examiner. The polygraph requirement should be broached at that time. When
this method is used with an agent who really wants to weasel out of a polygraph test, the following excuse is not uncommon: "Gentlemen, I'd love to take the test tonight, but
unfortunately I can only stay for fifteen minutes. I have an
important engagement I have to run off to."

The second school of thought believes that the case officer should tell the agent in advance in order to secure his
agreement and assurance that he has sufficient time for the
interview. At that time, the location of the testing site should
be withheld from the agent. The case officer should meet
the agent before the examination and escort him to the site
where the polygrapher is waiting. Once again, an agent who
wants to weasel out of a polygraph test will simply fail to
meet the case officer. Both methods require that some vital information be kept from the agent: either the fact that
an examination is going to take place or the exact location
of the examination.

I once tested a surveillance team in tandem, one team
member after the other, for a case officer in a Southeast
Asian city. The team was composed of five men. All were
witting that they were employed by American intelligence,
all were witting that they were going to be polygraph tested,

and all knew the hotel where the tests were to be administered. The case officer had instructed each to meet him in the hotel lobby at different times of the day. The first two examinations were conducted without a hitch. The third examination took longer than anticipated, so the case officer was late meeting the fourth man in the lobby. During the fourth man's session, he responded quite dramatically to the issue of having revealed his secret relationship with American intelligence to unauthorized individuals. Subsequent interrogation on that issue elicited quite a few admissions from the asset. He was apparently the type of individual who was proud of his association with the Americans and saw nothing wrong with letting all his friends and acquaintances know about it. The concept of practicing good security was alien to him.

The most worrisome admission concerned a revelation he made just that day. While waiting in the lobby for the case officer to meet him, the asset apparently engaged the hotel desk clerk in conversation. During the conversation, he somehow thought it necessary and appropriate to mention that he was meeting his American intelligence boss in order to take a polygraph examination. When the case officer and I heard this, we closed out the session as quickly as we could, packed up, and left the hotel by a side entrance to avoid the lobby. Not knowing what the hotel desk clerk did with the information our man had blurted out, we felt it prudent to assume the worst and quickly vacate the premises.

The agent was the weak link that compromised the

security of our meeting arrangements. However, one weak link is all it takes to foil the clandestine nature of a covert polygraph test. Unfortunately, security seemed to be the last thing on the minds of office personnel during one of my TDYs to a South American capital city. A trainee and I had a rather large number of cases to conduct at the office. After our arrival, we discovered that a number of different case officers handled the agents. The trainee and I split up the caseload and set out to contact the officers, establish a schedule, review files, review meeting arrangements, etc. I had gone through this ritual dozens and dozens of times before, but this time it proved to be far from routine.

About an hour later, we regrouped and stared at each other for a moment before almost simultaneously blurting out, "They've all told their agents in advance both when and where their polygraph tests are going to be conducted."

I added, "Two of my case officers even tasked their agents with getting the hotel rooms for their own tests."

It just took a minimum amount of intelligence and a mere dash of common sense to realize that tradecraft of the worst kind had been applied to the meeting arrangements. In fact, one could say no tradecraft had been applied. Realizing that this was a potentially dangerous situation for us, the visiting polygraphers, we marched off to see the chief.

Luckily, he was readily available, and we were able to meet with him before proceeding any further with our preparation to conduct the cases. After the two of us entered his office, I proceeded to tell him what we had discovered during our meetings with the case officers. I fully expected him to get angry over the sloppy work of his officers or to make some kind of excuse for their failure to make secure meeting arrangements.

Instead, smiling broadly, he said, "Well, yes, I know."

I was stunned, but I was all ears.

He continued, "We held a meeting several weeks ago in preparation for your visit and decided it would be a tremendous show of trust if we were to be open and aboveboard like this. We didn't want to spring it on them. It seemed to be the best thing to do to maintain good relations with our agents."

I paused long enough to make sure he was not going to break out laughing at the joke he just made. I was hoping he would double over with convulsive laughter and say, "Ha! Gotcha!"

When I was sure he was serious, in a calm voice I said, "Well, let's consider the worst-case scenario. We know that the reason for us being here is to help you determine whether your agents are good or bad. It sounds like you think you know the answer to that already, but let's assume for a second that one agent may be bad and has been reporting to the local intelligence service on all contacts he has had with his case officer. Now he knows that a visitor from Washington is in town to conduct a polygraph test. He has undoubtedly passed this information on to the local service as well. If the local service decided to end their operation against the case officer in order to arrest us all, don't you think this would be the ideal time? By giving the meeting information to them in advance, we are making it extremely easy for them. They could catch both the case officer and the visiting examiner in a very embarrassing and compromising situation with the agent, as well as seize the polygraph equipment. Wouldn't that be a politically embarrassing story of U.S. espionage activities in this country and wouldn't that make a nice picture on the front page of tomorrow morning's newspaper? I'm sure the U.S. government does not want it publicized that we were caught red-handed recruiting the citizens here to spy on the local government for us."

Of course, he saw the logic of my argument and agreed that the meeting arrangements could be handled using better tradecraft, but I'm not really sure he grasped just how idiotic their decision to be open and aboveboard had been. It is almost incomprehensible that the case officers, the chief, and whoever else attended that meeting all thought it was a good idea to throw sound tradecraft out the window. I believe they had all been lulled into a false sense of security. At least the chief listened to reason and finally made sure that the meetings were all rescheduled so the agents would not know either when or where their tests were going to be conducted.

All of the cases were safely and successfully conducted at that office. Unfortunately, there were occasions when case officers at other offices grew lax, developed a false sense of security, and operated in a reckless manner, jeopardizing my career goal of staying out of a foreign prison. I often wondered how basic operational tradecraft could be so ignored by the very professionals who use it the most. I encountered another situation involving lax security during a South American swing with yet a different trainee, Phil. Phil was on his first overseas trip to conduct operational polygraph cases. We were at our last stop on a six-week swing through South America. We had already traveled in and out of five different countries and had conducted many cases together. At the beginning of the trip, Phil watched as I conducted the first few cases, and I watched him conduct the next several. From that point on in the TDY, we were both operating independently. I had a break in my schedule one day at our last stop, so I decided to accompany Phil on his case one afternoon.

The case officer escorted us to a hotel room he had secured for the conduct of the test. As Phil started to set up the polygraph instrument, I noticed the case officer sitting comfortably in an easy chair watching us. I continued to watch Phil at work setting up the polygraph equipment, but I also kept glancing at the case officer in the easy chair. I thought it was close to the time Phil told me the case was scheduled to begin and thought it curious that the case officer was not on his way to meet the agent. My suspicious nature started to get the better of me.

"Don't you have to leave soon to pick up the agent?" I asked the case officer.

I tried to make my question sound like one asked out of idle curiosity. I think I pulled it off. He answered without any concern in his reply.

"Nope. He's coming directly here in about a half hour," he replied calmly.

I digested his response for a moment while trying to suppress the growing fear that I was in the middle of yet another fouled-up agent meeting.

"So he thinks this is just going to be a regular meeting?"

"Nope. He knows he's going to be polygraphed during the meeting today," he answered, with no realization evident in his voice that there was anything wrong with his reply.

Phil overheard my conversation with the case officer. He stopped what he was doing. I looked over and noticed his head hanging down. He finally looked up at me with a rather sheepish look on his face.

Even though I knew what the answer would be, I still asked Phil, "Did you inquire about the meeting arrangements before we traveled out here today?"

"I must have forgotten to do it," he replied.

After a few moments of silence while I considered how to handle the situation, I ordered Phil to pack up the equipment.

"Pack it up," I directed. "Stow those attachments. Clean out that inkwell and flush out those pens. Gather your paperwork. We're leaving."

As I had hoped, my instructions caught the ear of the case officer. Like someone who just received an electric shock, he stood straight up and asked me what was wrong.

I told him, "There is absolutely no need for a polygraph test today. We're leaving."

"What? Why?" he asked.

I replied, "It's obvious to me that you have one hundred percent confidence and trust in your agent."

He beamed and said, "You're right."

"Well, not only do you completely trust your agent with your freedom and your life, you also trust him with our freedom and our lives. No polygraph test can give you any more confidence in your agent than you already have." I said, hoping that my anger and disdain were evident.

"Well, it's Headquarters that wants him tested," he said defensively.

I really had no desire to actually terminate the polygraph session. I hoped that my dramatics would get his attention and drive home the operational security points I was about to provide. Now that I had the case officer's undivided attention, I explained that if he was wrong and the agent had been reporting to the local service on his contacts with American intelligence, today's meeting might be the ideal time to wrap up their operation against us. They could arrest the case officer and two polygraphers, with the confiscated polygraph equipment being the icing on their cake.

To the case officer's credit, he listened to what I had to say and then went down to the hotel front desk. He complained about the room and made arrangements for us all to transfer to another room on another floor. Then he waited in the lobby to intercept the agent when he entered the hotel so he could escort him to the new room.

I can recall one other situation that occurred in Central America that was very similar. Once again, I decided to accompany a trainee on one of his cases near the end of our trip. This time I did not find out until the agent was in the room that he had been informed in advance of the exact location of his polygraph examination. I gave the case officer my scary speech about the worst-case scenario of being arrested and having our pictures in the morning paper. It seemed to make an impression on her. I believe she had never given any serious thought to something like that happening. When polygraph testing of her agent concluded with Deception Indicated results, she was visibly upset, no doubt as the result of my scary speech. As it turned out, she needlessly worried. We exited the hotel without incident after the polygraph session. On the other hand, I hope it was a lesson well learned, and I hope she gave basic tradecraft the attention it deserved during future polygraph examinations.

The advice I received from my training trip instructor was the same advice I gave trainees on the road: if you don't want to end up being the next U.S. government employee stuck in a foreign prison convicted of espionage, don't blindly place your safety and security in the hands of case officers. You must know their jobs almost as well as they do so that you can double-check on the security of meeting arrangements.

I have conducted many covert operational cases that

were simple and straightforward. They were professionally planned and skillfully carried out with all security and safety concerns addressed. That was not the case with one of my polygraph tests in Southeast Asia that turned into a bizarre, security nightmare.

It was scheduled in a hurry during one of my lengthy TDYs to the country. A case officer visited my desk one day and requested that I handle a case at one of the offices up-country. He advised that I move quickly in order to get reservations on the overnight train since airline flights to that location were few and far between. Always willing to see new places, I agreed to go, despite the rushed nature of the request. I set forth making all the necessary arrangements. A message was sent to the office, and I obtained contact instructions. I made reservations on a train departing at 7:00 P.M. with a scheduled arrival time of 5:00 A.M. the next morning. I was delightfully surprised to discover I was going to travel in a sleeping car, something I had never experienced before. I fondly recalled the James Bond movie, *From Russia with Love,* where Bond has a violent encounter with an assassin from SPECTRE while a beautiful girl lay asleep in the bed, drugged by the very same assassin. I thought, *Wow, this is going to be fun!*

I checked out of my hotel that evening and was met by a driver from the office who was instructed to help me board the right train at the city's train station. Arriving at the train station, I was thankful for the driver's help. I never would have found the right train without him. With the help of a porter, I was escorted to my room in the sleeping car. In broken English, the porter told me he would wake me in the morning and let me know when we reached our destination. I thanked both of them profusely and took stock of my surroundings.

It was nothing like James Bond's sleeping car, but it had character. It was small. Actually, it was tiny. There was a small bed, a small closet, and a small metal counter with a sink and a mirror. My expectations were not met, but I didn't care. It was romantic in a way, and it was both a new experience and a new way to travel. I settled in and started reading to pass the time but found the view outside to be more interesting. Once outside the city, the view of the countryside and small villages was absolutely stunning. Before long, nightfall obscured any decent view, so the only opportunity to actually see anything was when the train rolled through towns along the way.

As novel and romantic as travel in that manner was, there were numerous distractions that made sleeping in the room nearly impossible. First, it was bumpy. The train car pitched, swayed, and bounced its way down the tracks for hours on end. Next, it was noisy. The knocks, bangs, and clangs were nonstop. The train must have pulled in and out of twenty to thirty different stations during the night. Each stop brought the noise of people boarding and disembarking, and the train itself made a great deal of noise each time it pulled in and out of a station. The brakes squealed, and the clangs and screeches were deafening. I may have dozed a bit, but I read most of the night and watched the limited scenery out the window.

I awoke, shaved, and dressed long before I was notified my stop was approaching. Within minutes, I was dragging my suitcase down the steps, across the tracks, and onto a dirt path that led to the train station several hundred feet away. It was a very long train and the sleeping car was at the end of the train. I stood and watched people descend from the train and greet relatives and friends who came to meet them. I knew that I was supposed to be met at the station. I assumed I would be met by one of the officers who were assigned to the office, but I didn't see any Caucasian faces in the crowd anywhere. I also didn't see any taxis anywhere. It was 5:00 A.M. I stuck out like a sore thumb, but not knowing what else to do, I just stood there and waited. I was finally approached by an indigenous individual who said he was sent to take me to my hotel. I assumed the gentleman who graciously met me at five o'clock in the morning was a driver from the office. He drove me to my hotel and then accompanied me as I entered the hotel with luggage in hand. As I checked in at the front desk and started to register, the clerk put two room keys on the counter.

"No," I said. "Just one room will do for me."

"Your reservation is for two rooms," he said.

The driver then chimed in and said he was the one who telephoned the hotel to make my reservation and that he had been instructed to reserve two rooms. I was in no position to argue, so I finished registering for the two rooms. The driver said someone from the office planned to meet me at ten o'clock in the morning, and I thought, *Fine, I'll straighten out this business of the two rooms with him at that time.* I thanked the driver for his help and then carted my luggage to my two rooms.

The case officer knocked on my door at 10 A.M. We exchanged greetings and he entered the room. I was surprised to see the driver with him. The driver entered, too. Also, I noticed that the case officer carried a brown briefcase. It looked suspiciously like a polygraph instrument to me, but I knew that it very well could have been a real briefcase.

"Well, here is your subject and here is your polygraph instrument," the case officer said. "Are you going to use this room or the other room?"

I was stunned. There were so many things wrong with the situation that I did not know where to begin.

I had to start somewhere, so I said, "Now I know why you wanted me to register for two rooms. Do you realize that my travel orders do not permit me to pay for operational expenses? I can't get reimbursed for renting two rooms. Operational expenses fall on your shoulders."

"Really?" he said. "No problem. I'll pay for one of the rooms. I'll arrange it with the front desk."

"Okay." I said. "Do you realize you've just compromised my true identity to your man here by having him pick me up at the train station, having him reserve my room at this hotel, and bringing him to my room to be tested?"

"Alan," he said. "There is no protecting your identity here. This place is too small. Everyone knows who you are already. And this gentleman here has been our man at the office for years now."

"Look," I replied. "That may be true, but let's not make

it easy for the opposition. Let's try to do this thing right. Please, send him on his way and tell him you'll get in touch with him later. Take me to the office. I know you brought the instrument with you, but I'd like to check it out and calibrate it properly, preferably not in front of the person I'm going to test. Also, I'd like to discuss the case with you, review the files, and prepare a list of polygraph test questions for your concurrence. I know we're out in the field here, and we can play this thing fast and loose, but let's follow standard operating procedure as best we can. Okay?"

He reluctantly agreed, and I thought I picked up a hint of disappointment as if I had caught him with his hand in the cookie jar. I began to feel like he was trying to play me for a sucker.

When we arrived at the office, I checked out the polygraph equipment while the case officer handled some of his business. Then I asked for the file on the agent. He handed me several documents that contained personal history questionnaire information. I read the documents he provided and took notes, but I finished with them in just a few minutes.

"Wait a minute," I said. "You told me the agent has worked for the office for years. Surely you have a file on him?"

He hesitated for a moment, as if trying to decide what to do next, but without saying a word he walked several feet to a safe and flipped through some files before extracting one that he handed to me. I took a while to digest the data.

When I was finished, I confronted the case officer, "There is a reference in the file to a previous polygraph test, but there is no summary cable or final polygraph report that describes the outcome of the test. Important information like that must be kept on file here, too. Right?"

Once again I caught that hint of disappointment in his expression.

"It must be in the other file," he muttered.

He went back to the safe and flipped through a few more files before extracting another file (a much thicker file this time).

"Is that all of it now?" I challenged. "Is there any more information on file about the agent that I don't have?"

He shook his head, and with a sheepish and sorrowful look, turned to busy himself with work. I proceeded to review the rest of the material. It quickly became evident why the case officer tried to rush the case—why he did not want me to prepare for it—why he tried to keep information from me. The agent had been polygraphed before and the results of the examination were unfavorable—Deception Indicated. There were strong indications that he had revealed his relationship with us to unauthorized people and that he was reporting to the host intelligence service. The agent had been interrogated at length by the last examiner, but no significant admissions had been obtained. I could have rubbed the case officer's nose in his shenanigans, but I realized that little would be gained by taking that course of action. The best course of action seemed to be to handle the case to the best of my ability.

The agent's test was eventually conducted later that day. Since it made little difference at that point, the test was conducted in the room adjoining mine at the hotel. Apparently, time did not sooth the agent's apprehensions. He reacted with even more strength and clarity than he had done during his previous polygraph test. I interrogated for a substantial amount of time but was unsuccessful in extracting the cause for his reactions. That came as no surprise, since the events prior to my examination provided the agent with little incentive to reveal the truth. After all, he had trouble with his last polygraph test and was interrogated at length, but he made no admissions during that session and nothing bad happened to him as a result. He still remained employed. He was still paid regularly, and the office made no change to his status or access. No action had been taken against him, and the relationship went on as before. Acting bewildered and denying any wrongdoing served him well during his last polygraph, and I'm sure he saw no reason to change tactics that served him so well in the past. Although I was certain the case officer tried to have the agent retested without affording me time to properly prepare for the test, and I was equally as certain he tried to conceal the agent's negative information from me; I never confronted the case officer with his high jinks.

I was unable to obtain a confession. The case officer was very unhappy with the Deception Indicated results in my report of the polygraph interview and interrogation. I'm sure he was concerned that Headquarters was going to order that his working relationship with the agent be terminated. I hope that they did.

I have often compared the polygraph process to a medical doctor's efforts to reach a diagnosis. A doctor first asks a patient to provide a complete medical history. He then interviews the patient, asking about all the problems and symptoms the patient is currently experiencing. He then performs an examination and finally orders specific scientific medical tests related to the problems he has identified. The doctor's diagnosis is made after considering all of the information available to him. There is little doubt the accuracy of a doctor's diagnosis would lessen if a patient simply said, "Doc, I'm not going to tell you about my medical history. I'm not going to tell you about my current problems or allow you to examine me. Just order your scientific tests and tell me what, if anything, is wrong with me." Obviously, information from the patient's medical history, current symptoms, and physical examination guide the doctor to specific tests that will aid him in making his final diagnosis.

The polygraph process is not dissimilar. The examiner uses a "whole person" concept to make his diagnosis of Deception Indicated, No Deception Indicated, or Inconclusive. In order to formulate the appropriate test questions and in order to ask the appropriate questions during interrogations, the examiner should have all of the background information available. Withholding this information from the examiner drastically weakens the precision and accuracy of the polygraph process.

There was one final oddity that occurred. I still don't understand it to this day. I made reservations to fly back to the capital city from the local airport. On my day of departure, my hotel front desk flatly refused to reserve a taxi for me. They said that taxis were not permitted to drive to the airport. I couldn't believe my ears, but the front desk was quite insistent. I called the case officer at the office, and he agreed to personally pick me up at the hotel to drive me to the airport. When he arrived at the hotel, I was surprised to learn he apparently decided at the last minute to travel with me. We were both on the flight that day.

On the flight back, I had a window seat. I gazed out the window for almost the entire flight reflecting on what an experience that "routine" case had been and how safety and security concerns were so ignored by the case officer.

Security was always on my mind while traveling. In the world of covert operations, I made decisions daily regarding operational security issues, such as the selection of testing locations, the notification of an agent about a polygraph test, or the implementation of counter-surveillance measures. To operate in foreign countries, I had to decide on travel routes to the office, how to keep a low profile in my manner of dress and conduct of my daily activities, and how to protect classified information and equipment. We all make decisions every day, and we try our hardest to make sure they are good decisions. It's usually in our best interest to do so. Good decisions are the best ones, bad decisions are the worst, and incredibly stupid decisions should be avoided like the bubonic plague. Unfortunately, I've been inoculated against the bubonic plague, but not against making exceedingly stupid decisions.

On one of my visits to the capital city in Southeast Asia, I took a side trip up-country in order to conduct four operational cases for the office. It was a city I had never traveled to before, so I welcomed the opportunity to visit. When I did a little advance research with fellow officers on what the city had to offer, I discovered that the airport had a reputation of being dangerous. When my flight approached the landing strip, I realized why. As the plane made its last turn for its final approach, I watched as people, carts, oxen, goats, and chickens scurried across the strip trying to beat the fast approaching plane. It was a comical but extremely dangerous scene.

The work I performed for the office was uneventful. I had a pleasant visit, and all the meeting arrangements were professionally handled. The conduct of the four cases for the office was accomplished in about four days. When the work was done, I needed to return to handle more cases for the office in the capital city. The transport of polygraph equipment and case materials was usually accomplished by sending them through official channels, but when I discussed this option with the chief, he advised that the service was very infrequent. If I used the official channels, my equipment wouldn't leave for over a week. I wouldn't be able to finalize my reports or use the equipment for the pending work, and I would be stuck in the country for a long time in a holding pattern. The chief recommended that I hand-carry the materials on the flight back. His recommendation might sound outlandish today, but security concerns in those days didn't include worries of airport security checks. They weren't performed in those days. So, all of the charts, notes, and question lists for the four operational cases were placed in envelopes, and I then placed the envelopes in the lid of the polygraph instrument.

Despite my unorthodox luggage, the trip back was relatively uneventful. There was no security check at the airport. The briefcase with the polygraph built inside and with the envelopes stuffed in the lid probably weighed about twenty-five pounds, so it was annoying to have to tote it along with my other luggage. The airport was small, crowded, and hot. Upon arrival at the capital city, I took a taxi from the airport back to the hotel I was fond of patronizing. It was within walking distance of the office.

It was a long, hot taxi ride, but when I arrived at the hotel, the bellboy spied the taxi at the curb and came running down the steps to assist with my luggage. My large suitcase was in the trunk of the taxi, and I had the briefcase beside me on the backseat. The taxi driver hefted my suitcase out of the trunk for me as I stood beside him. He placed it on the sidewalk as I pulled the wallet out of my back pocket to pay him. I certainly could have carried my own luggage up the steps into the hotel, but since the bellboy had graciously hopped down the steps to the curb to aid a weary traveler, I elected to give him the tip he was looking for. Since I was more or less obligated to tip the bellboy to carry my suitcase, I decided to let the bellboy carry the heavy briefcase as well. After all, it was hot, and the briefcase was heavy. I set the briefcase down next to the suitcase on the sidewalk. After I paid the taxi driver and started up the steps to the hotel, I glanced over my shoulder and saw the bellboy bend over to grab my luggage. As I entered the hotel I walked to the front desk and again glanced back to make sure the bellboy was behind me. He had followed me up the steps and through the front entrance, and I saw him bend over as he placed my luggage near the elevator. I finished with the registration process at the front desk and then walked over to the bellboy.

I saw four or five suitcases near the elevator. To remind the bellboy, I pointed toward my luggage.

I said, "Two bags," and started for the elevator.

He said, "No. One bag."

I stopped in my tracks, turned, and said, "No. Two bags."

My eyes nervously darted around in search of my two pieces of luggage. The bellboy stood next to my suitcase, but the briefcase that contained a polygraph instrument with materials from four top secret covert cases was nowhere in sight. Fearing the worst, I sped through the lobby, flung the front doors open, and bounded down to the sidewalk taking three or four steps at a time. Miraculously, the briefcase was still sitting there on the sidewalk where I set it down, and people were actually stepping around it as they walked down the sidewalk. Overwhelmed by my good fortune, I snatched up the briefcase and felt a rush of relief as my heart actually started beating again. What a close call. What an idiot I was. Whatever possessed me to think it was a good decision to allow a foreign national to carry the polygraph instrument and materials from four top secret operational cases? Discovery of that information could have led to incarceration or death. Frankly, it is simply astonishing that no one stole the briefcase in the time it took me to register at the front desk. I cannot begin to imagine the trouble I would have been in if the briefcase had been gone when I ran back down to the sidewalk. How would I have explained my decision to let the briefcase out of my hands and out of my sight? Saying, "It was hot," certainly wouldn't have been adequate. Saying, "I wanted to get the most out of my fifty-cent tip," wouldn't have been any better.

I kept this unflattering story to myself for many, many years. I was overwhelmed with embarrassment and felt like the south end of a north-bound horse. I always prided myself on being a world-traveling security officer, a polygraph professional, and one who had devoted much of his career trying to teach others about safety and security issues during the conduct of covert polygraph cases. Unfortunately, on that day, there was a stupid contest, and I was the grand prize winner.

Chapter Eighteen

Best Laid Plans

Honesty is the best policy.
— MIGUEL DE CERVANTES SAAVEDRA

W hen making arrangements for a covert ops polygraph examination of an agent, I tried to think of all contingencies to make the meeting safe. Threats to my safety came in many forms. Surveillance was one threat. Surveillance is employed by foreign intelligence services for a variety of reasons. It can be used to verify whether Americans are actually intelligence officers. A suspected intelligence officer may be followed to find out where he goes, what he does, and whom he sees. There is another type of surveillance employed by foreign intelligence services that is equally as annoying. It is surveillance designed to worry or harass the target of the surveillance. Those performing the surveillance don't care whether they are discovered by the target. In fact, they may wish to be discovered because their aim is to pester and harass to the point of preventing the target from doing anything clandestine. This is their way of saying, "We see what you're doing. You're not so smart." Or "Watch out! Be careful! We can nab you any time we want to." Or "Better not do anything wrong. We're watching you."

One of my favorite capital cities in South America is a very cosmopolitan city. It is an enormous metropolis with a mixture of cultures over the centuries that has produced a city of fascinating people, buildings of splendid architectural design, and an abundance of entertainment activities to keep a visitor busy during any idle time he is fortunate enough to have. I had the pleasure of visiting the city many times. The office was a prolific user of the polygraph to vet its agents, and I could usually count on it to have quite a few agents scheduled for testing during our routine swings through the continent. It was a good stop on our South American training trips. Those swings through the continent would typically involve handling cases in five to six countries per trip. During training trips, I usually conducted the first case or two so that the other examiner could watch me from beginning to end. The "trainees" on training trips were always experienced, competent examiners. Some had even traveled overseas before for other jobs. The multi-stop trips were "training trips" in the sense that they were examiners' first trips conducting covert operations polygraph cases in foreign countries. I usually conducted the first case involving the use of an interpreter so the trainee could watch me. After several cases, I split the workload evenly with the trainee. Our work schedule at each office frequently permitted us to accompany each other as we conducted cases.

On my first day at the office in this city with another examiner, Sam, we were briefed on the threat of surveillance by the local intelligence service. We were advised there was a current campaign to surveil Americans in our building, especially those known or suspected to be intelligence officers. We were also told that the surveillance teams were using light blue sedans.

We started our polygraph work at the office and were appreciative of all the tradecraft used by the case officers for the conduct of the examinations. Each of us had conducted several examinations during our first week there at the office without a hitch. Neither we nor the case officers noted any surveillance. Regrettably, our good fortune did not last.

Sam had an afternoon case scheduled, and as I happened to be caught up in my report writing, I decided to accompany him. I learned that the case officer wanted us to meet him at a certain street corner in the city at two o'clock that afternoon. He planned to drive his personal vehicle to another location in the city and then flag down a taxi. He was going to have the taxi stop at our street corner at two o'clock and then have the three of us proceed in another taxi.

Sam and I had lunch at the cafeteria and then left the building. With two hours of free time before we had to be at the meeting point, we decided we had ample time for a healthy, long walk and a bit of sightseeing. It proved to be a very pleasant two hours, and we didn't notice anything unusual during our walk.

We arrived at the street corner at the appointed time and waited five or ten minutes before the case officer arrived in a taxi. After he exited the taxi and paid the driver, we talked for a minute while the taxi drove away. The case officer then flagged down another taxi, and we all entered. As the case officer provided our destination to the taxi driver, Sam noticed a light blue sedan drive up and stop right behind our taxi.

As our taxi pulled away from the curb and entered the flow of traffic, the light blue sedan followed right behind us. After traveling several blocks and noticing that the light blue sedan continued to follow right behind us, Sam brought it to the attention of the case officer. With a flick-of-a-wrist gesture, he dismissed it as a coincidence. After several more city blocks of travel that included a number of turns, the light blue sedan could still be found right behind us. I thought the situation to be curious, certainly not one to be so easily dismissed as a coincidence. I wasn't overly concerned, as I knew the case officer had additional changes planned in our travel to the testing site, a safe house in the suburbs. I may not have been worried, but I noticed that Sam was a little nervous. He was a bit fidgety and kept glancing back at the light blue sedan. No doubt he was recalling some of the spooky stories I told him over a few cold beers during our trip together.

The next stop on our route to the safe house was one of the city's subway stations. The taxi pulled over to the curb on the opposite side of the street from the subway station entrance. The case officer exited the taxi and paid the driver while the two of us climbed out of the backseat. As we stepped onto the sidewalk, the light blue sedan pulled up behind our taxi and stopped. The driver got out of the car, approached the wall of the building next to us, and stared with great intensity at a poster plastered on the wall. As I glanced over at the poster, I realized how ridiculous his behavior was, because the poster was one that had been plastered on the wall many, many years ago. About 60 percent of it was worn or ripped away. It was actually illegible. I could think of no logical reason in the world why anyone would stop at the curb, exit their vehicle, and walk over to read that poster.

The case officer ushered us across the street to the subway station entrance. Once we reached the other side of the street, I glanced back and saw that the light blue sedan was no longer there. An escalator ride down to the station took us to the booth where the case officer purchased tokens for us all, and then he led us past several platforms before directing us toward a particular subway car. As I sat down, I selected a seat that allowed me to watch the comings and goings of anyone in our car, as well as the car ahead of us. I did not see the "poster" man or anyone else I thought was suspicious in any way. As we sat in the subway car waiting for its departure, Sam once again brought up the topic of surveillance by the light blue sedan.

The case officer acted surprised and said, "Surveillance? What surveillance? No, you guys are mistaken. There was no surveillance on us."

Well, I guess we wouldn't have known for sure unless the man in the light blue sedan had walked up to us and said, "Hi. My name is Juan. I've been assigned to follow you guys today. Nice to meet you."

Since it was unlikely for that to occur, I thought it was prudent for us to consider the circumstances of the light blue sedan to be suspicious. For reasons I failed to grasp, the case officer did not.

After traveling for a half hour, we arrived at a subway station stop in the suburbs on the other side of the city. We left the station, and the case officer led us on a walk through the streets of a housing area. There were many pedestrians around the station, but as we got farther into the neighborhoods, we seemed to be all alone. I kept checking to see if we were being followed by foot or by car. I didn't notice anything suspicious. Soon my mind moved on to more pleasant thoughts as the case officer ushered us into a nice house on a cul-de-sac located in a quiet neighborhood.

The house was old and rather large. Immediately upon entering the front door, we encountered stairs that led up to the second floor where the living room and kitchen were located. There was a small breakfast table in the kitchen area that was ideal for the conduct of the examination. The examiner and I shared the chore of setting up the polygraph equipment in the kitchen. From the kitchen table, I glimpsed the case officer lounging in the living room. I walked over and talked with him while the examiner looked at his notes and question lists in preparation for the interview. I asked some basic questions about the agent and was told that the two of them had their regularly scheduled meetings at the safe house.

"Well, you've got a great place to meet here. It's comfortable enough, but it's also so wonderfully quiet. This is fantastic," I said.

"You're right. We've never been disturbed here. Quiet as a church mouse," he replied.

The agent arrived at the appointed time. After all the introductions were made and an explanation for our presence was given, he readily agreed to take the polygraph examination. The case officer remained in the living room, out of sight and out of earshot. The examiner and the agent seated themselves at the breakfast table, and I sat to one side to observe.

The interview progressed smoothly and was at a point when the agent was connected to the instrument by the three sensors, when quite unexpectedly, the doorbell rang. It was a horribly loud noise. It sounded like a fire alarm— an ultra-loud *clang, clang, clang*. I jumped out of my chair and out of my skin at the same time. My thoughts immediately raced back to the blue sedan we encountered earlier. Sam stopped in the middle of reading a polygraph test question and froze in place. The case officer leaped out of the living room and started bounding down the stairs three at a time to see who was at the door. The agent began pulling the sensors off in preparation to fight or flee.

"Get that instrument packed up now. Quick!" I snapped at Sam.

We were all in shock and our nerves were frayed. Sam's efforts rivaled those of a one-armed, nearsighted monkey. There was no time to properly pack up the polygraph instrument. There was no time to flush the ink out of pens, to empty the community inkwell in a sink, or to fold and store components away in their little compartments. Sam hurriedly placed all the accessories, notes, and charts on top of the instrument's faceplate and tried to close the lid. It would not close. Rubber tubing kept flipping out, preventing the lid from shutting.

In utter frustration, he threw up his hands and said, "I can't do it. It won't close."

I started to laugh a little, but I was not laughing at Sam. I believe the sudden tension thrust upon all of us made me laugh out of nervousness more than anything else. Then again, there was certainly no escaping the fact that we all looked very silly in those few seconds. I went to the window to see if I could detect anything unusual outside. The cul-de-sac looked quiet and serene, exactly as it appeared when we arrived. When I returned to Sam's side to assist with the instrument, the case officer came rushing back upstairs to inform us that we had merely been visited by a door-to-door salesman. You could feel the tension leave the room as if someone had released a steam valve. All four of us sat down and breathed a sigh of relief.

Once again, I thought I was on the verge of being carted away to a foreign prison, only to discover that a set of

unusual, but benign, circumstances had been misinter-
preted. On the other hand, maybe the harassment surveillance earlier in the day had accomplished exactly what it
had intended to do. It put us on edge, frayed our nerves,
and made it more difficult to do what we set out to do.

Obviously, meetings with recruited agents in foreign
countries are arranged to be as safe and clandestine as possible. However, when a covert operations polygraph case is
conducted in the United States, tradecraft is still employed
as if the case were being conducted in a foreign country.
The same goal of completing the case in a safe and clandestine fashion applies because the relationship between the
agent and the Agency is a secret. All parties involved want
to keep the relationship secret. The biggest threat is the potential commotion caused by being discovered by police, hotel management, apartment building managers, private
security officials, or members of the media. The case officer, the polygraph examiner, and the agent all want to keep
low profiles. All want to complete a polygraph interview
here in the United States without being detained or questioned by anyone. So, even though we are on home soil,
we ensure polygraph interviews are conducted in a safe and
clandestine manner.

One of the cases I conducted in the Washington DC
area turned out to be anything but routine. There was nothing remarkable about the agent or his relationship with the
Agency. He was an asset who had been developed, recruited,
and handled in a foreign country, but had yet to be poly-

graphed to establish his bona fides. Since he was in the Washington DC area on a business trip, the decision was made to afford him the opportunity to be tested here. A case officer at Headquarters had been assigned to meet with the agent during his visit. I had ample time at Headquarters to prepare for the examination. I reviewed the files in the case officer's office and discussed the case with him. I prepared the test questions to be utilized during the examination and had them approved by the case officer. The agent's English was excellent, so I did not require the services of an interpreter.

In my discussions with the case officer, I discovered that the arrangements for the polygraph interview were well thought out. The examination was going to be conducted in one of Washington's large hotels. I was instructed to meet the case officer in the hotel lobby at ten o'clock in the morning. He planned to escort me to the room, and after I set up the polygraph equipment, he would make his way down to the lobby to meet the agent and escort him to the room. As far as I was concerned, the arrangements should have permitted the secure conduct of the polygraph interview— providing no unforeseen events interfered. However, the unexpected has a way of interfering with the best laid plans.

The day of the examination was an absolutely gorgeous Washington fall day with cool temperatures and low humidity. Its beauty was marred by an absolutely horrendous commute into the city. I lived in the Virginia suburbs, about twenty-five miles from Washington, and I encountered bumper-to-bumper traffic most of the way. However, I have always been one to try to plan ahead and anticipate the unforeseen. I departed my residence in plenty of time to fight the traffic, find parking, and be in the lobby of the hotel at the agreed upon time. The case officer was waiting there when I arrived. He escorted me to a bank of elevators and took me to the hotel room secured for the polygraph interview.

We entered the room together. I took a quick look around at the accommodations and decided that a small sitting area in the corner of the room was the best place to set up the equipment. I moved items around on the table to make room for the polygraph instrument and started to prepare for the interview. As I glanced around the hotel room, I noticed that the bed looked like it had been slept in. There was an alarm clock on the nightstand, as well as toiletries in the bathroom. There were clothes hanging in the closet, shoes on the floor, and a suitcase on the bed. When I first entered the room I thought that the case officer must have stayed in the room the night before, but now I saw him standing at the edge of the bed staring at the suitcase.

I walked over to him and asked, "What's going on?"

He replied, "I'm not sure. Someone in my office rented this hotel room yesterday and passed the keys to me at the office early this morning. All this stuff in here is what's bothering me. I just can't imagine him going to such elaborate lengths. Look at the tag on the suitcase. It's got a foreign name and a South African address on it. Look at this Bible on the nightstand. It seems to be written in Afrikaans."

I agreed it seemed unlikely that such meticulous measures had been taken. Also, it was worrisome that the luggage tag did not match the name of the individual who rented the room. The case officer decided to call the front desk. He did his best to explain the situation, but found it difficult to find the right words to explain that he had rented a room, only to find out that someone else may have moved into it while he was out. When he finally made himself understood, the case officer blanched as he heard how excited the front desk became over news that we were in a room occupied by another guest. He quickly hung up the phone and told me to pack up the equipment as fast as I could.

"They must think we're burglars or something," he said. "They're coming right up here to find out what's going on. Hurry, Alan. We've got to get out of here!"

I didn't want to be questioned by house detectives or hotel managers any more than the case officer, so I hurriedly packed up my equipment. We both made a hasty retreat. As we fled down the hallway, the case officer told me he would contact me at my office to reschedule the examination. We split up. I went one way to make my way back to Headquarters, and the case officer made his way to the lobby to meet the agent.

That was the only time in my life I have known a hotel

to double-rent a room by mistake. We were fortunate that we were able to vacate the premises before hotel management arrived, and we were even more fortunate that the other occupant of the room did not return while we were inside. Even when you try as hard as you can, unforeseen events can interfere with plans to maintain secrecy.

Chapter Nineteen

One Interpreter Too Many

If there was twenty ways of telling the truth
and only one way of telling a lie, the
Government would find it out. It's in the
nature of governments to tell lies.
                    —GEORGE BERNARD SHAW

Communication between two people can be a
horrifically difficult task to accomplish at times. Selective hearing occurs routinely during the course
of even normal conversation. Portions of conversation are
consciously or unconsciously tuned out, usually by both
parties. Misinterpretations and misunderstandings occur
frequently, resulting in consequences that range from hurt
feelings to war being declared.

Not all translation problems happen abroad. One of my

worst communication failures happened on a summer job in southern Virginia, where all parties spoke the same language. Some of my coworkers had thick accents with a drawl to their speech that made it difficult to understand them at times. I thought my ear was pretty well attuned to their speech patterns, and I usually didn't have any problem understanding them, but that proved to be far from true one hot summer afternoon. As I sauntered up to a truck to climb into the backseat, I noticed one of the older, native Virginians sitting in the front seat.

As I approached, he looked down at me and said something that sounded like, "Wufta tuneeda snik otto inda forno oppa tu?"

I couldn't understand a single word he said. He might as well have been speaking to me in a foreign language. From the intonation in his voice, I was almost certain he was posing a question, but that was all I could discern from the words he spoke.

Stalling for time while I processed his words to try to make sense of something he uttered, I looked up at him and said, "Say what?"

He repeated, "Wufta tuneeda snik otto inda forno oppa tu?"

Not one word he said sounded like any English word I was familiar with. My ears passed the sounds to my brain, but my brain drew a total blank. His question was totally incomprehensible.

But the man in the truck must have been speaking English!

I cocked an eyebrow to show I was perplexed and said again, "Say what?"

He now had a disturbed look on his face. In a condescending, slow, and deliberate manner he repeated, "Wufta tuneeda snik otto inda forno oppa tu?"

Once again, his uttering was absolutely meaningless. I was both perplexed and uncomfortable. I was too embarrassed to tell him I couldn't understand him at all. Believing I had a fifty-fifty chance of giving the correct answer to his question, in an act of desperation I finally replied, "Yep."

He looked at me strangely and asked with a very puzzled look, "Yep?"

Based on his reaction, I knew I had given the wrong answer so I stalled once again by asking, "Uh, say what?"

"Wufta tuneeda snik otto inda forno oppa tu?" he said.

This time I confidently and emphatically answered, "Nope."

He looked at me as if I were some strange thing on the bottom of his shoe and said, "Nope?"

Now I was thoroughly embarrassed, confused, and extremely uncomfortable, so I said one more time, "Uh, say what?"

He stared at me for what seemed like an eternity and then with perhaps a little less slur this time repeated, "Wufta tuneeda snik otto inda forno oppa tu?"

There still was no English word in there as far as I could tell.

Seeking to put an end to this extremely discomforting and embarrassing situation, I simply said, "I don't know."

I turned my back to him and quickly walked away, still uncomfortable and confused. I'm sure he was bewildered by our exchange. I could feel his eyes burning into the back of my head as I walked away. I avoided him for the rest of the day and never did find out what he was saying.

If the art of communication can be so difficult between two English-speaking Americans, imagine the problems that can arise when one individual is a foreign national who speaks English as a second language or when an interpreter is required during a polygraph interview. There are times when I would prefer to use an interpreter rather than speak directly to an examinee who speaks English as a second language. Mangled English can be awfully difficult to understand.

When considering the use of an interpreter, there is also the added problem of his trustworthiness. If the examiner cannot understand a single word being said by either the examinee or the interpreter, how can he be sure that the interpreter is accurately passing on what is being said? Although it was not an absolute guarantee of trustworthiness, only polygraph-cleared interpreters were utilized in the conduct of covert operations polygraph examinations.

Control over the interview is another issue. It's imperative for the polygraph examiner to maintain control of the interview, but difficulties can arise because the interpreter is the vital link between the examiner and the examinee. Does the interpreter's important role put him in the driver's seat? In order to illustrate the potential problem with this issue of control, when training examiners in the use of interpreters I used to tell the following joke:

When the mafia searched for a new thug to make weekly collections of protection money extorted from New York City businesses, they decided to hire a man who didn't speak English. Constantly trying to outwit the police, they reasoned that if the man got caught, he wouldn't be able to communicate what he was doing.

During his first week on the job, the new thug proved to be an excellent collector of extortion money. He was a natural shakedown artist who was very good at pressuring the businesses to pay for protection. He collected over $500,000. Holding such a large amount of cash, the thug got greedy. He decided to keep the money and ended up hiding it instead of turning it over to the mafia.

Realizing they'd been stiffed, the mafia sent a couple of hoods after their new collector. Even though he was in hiding, he was quickly found by the hoods. They politely asked him where he had the money, but since he couldn't speak English, he couldn't answer them. The hoods couldn't communicate with him. The hoods hauled the collector off to an interpreter.

One of the hoods said to the interpreter, "Ask him where the money is."

"Where is the money?" the interpreter asked the collector.

The collector replied, "I don't know what you're talking about. And you can eat dirt and die!"

The interpreter told the hood, "He said he doesn't know what you're talking about. He also said you can eat dirt and die."

With cold eyes and an evil smile, the hood pulled out a gun and held it to the collector's forehead. He had fire in his belly and steel in his spine. It was obvious he was a man who was ready, willing, and able to pull the trigger.

"NOW ask him where the money is, one last time," he said to the interpreter.

"One last time, where is the money?" the interpreter asked.

The new collector began to sweat and started to shake uncontrollably. Glaring wide-eyed at the gun, he said, "The money is in Central Park. I buried it five feet to the right of the fountain at the West Fifty-sixth Street entrance."

"What did he say?" asked the hood.

The interpreter replied, "He said he still doesn't know what you are talking about and doesn't think you have the guts to pull that trigger."

The interpreter's trustworthiness is vital. He has the potential to control the polygraph interview and interrogation in ways that would greatly displease the polygraph examiner, if he were aware of it. I always made sure an interpreter I used was polygraph cleared. I also ensured an interpreter completely understood his role during the polygraph and interrogation process.

Although the interpreter has a vital role in helping me to communicate with an agent, my job of effectively utilizing an interpreter in the polygraph process is more complex. Good communication is essential. After all, everything I say to a polygraph examinee can influence the outcome of an examination. Everything I say is said for a purpose: to inform, to explain, to convince, to persuade, to reassure, or to elicit information. When significant portions of what I say are not accurately translated, I must question whether the examinee is receiving a fair test and whether the test results are valid. When utilizing an interpreter, I usually talk in short or partial sentences to make the interpreter's job easier and to ensure the examinee has the opportunity to hear my words translated accurately. If an interpreter is unable to repeat back in English, word for word, what I said, it would be impossible for him to translate my words with any accuracy.

Several years ago I monitored a polygraph interview that clearly demonstrated how this pairing of a polygraph interrogator and an interpreter is a relationship of mutual dependence. It only took several minutes of monitoring to realize that the examiner was either untrained or inexperienced in the conduct of examinations that required the services of an interpreter. At times, he spoke in multiple complex sentences, making it difficult, if not impossible, for the interpreter to translate accurately.

At one point, the examiner said something like, "But what I have the inability to do is to differentiate between those concerns, meaning I don't know if it's extremely significant and you went out and murdered a guy yesterday, or if it's other things that are concerning you. I don't know if you've gone out and had secret contact with various individuals that you intentionally didn't want to tell anybody about, or if you have other family members and friends who work in various work positions for whatever government."

Since I couldn't begin to repeat all those words back to the examiner in English, I felt the interpreter's attempt to translate them would surely be lacking.

Unfortunately, the examiner conducted much of the interview in similar fashion.

At another point in the interview, he said something like, "But how does any of that have anything to do with you? What is it about you, or your background, or what you've said, or what you've done, you are so concerned about, that you feel can impact this test today, or this job today, because most likely, you are creating something that is less significant than it really is?"

Sentences like those must make an interpreter's job a nightmare.

Obviously, this symbiotic relationship between interpreter and examiner requires skill on the part of both. My skill in this process was sorely put to the test during the conduct of a covert examination in Southeast Asia. Two interpreters were required. I have never heard of any examiner attempting to conduct an examination using two interpreters to communicate with an examinee. The agent to be tested was in contact with the CIA office because he wanted to inform on the location of a narcotics refinery in the Golden Triangle area. He lived in the mountains near the refinery and served as a mule, a carrier of narcotics, for the refinery. I believe he was a poor, uneducated man who had lived a hard life. He didn't speak Thai, Cambodian, Laotian, or English. He only spoke a mountain dialect indigenous to that area. The examinee was employed to transport narcotics from refineries. He had no shoes on when I met him, and his feet looked like blackened elephant leather. Based on his reaction to me when we met (slack-jawed and wide-eyed), I think I was the first Caucasian he ever encountered face-to-face. He was reporting on the location of a refinery out of revenge over something that was done or said to him by his employers at the refinery.

The office arranged for me to utilize the services of an interpreter who spoke the mountain dialect, but I learned I wouldn't be able to communicate with the interpreter directly because he couldn't speak English. The interpreter's second language was Thai. Completing the bridge for me to communicate with the agent, the office provided a second interpreter who spoke Thai and English. Although I would now be able to communicate with the agent, it was going to take a two-interpreter bridge to make it work.

This arrangement was certainly a novel approach, one that I had never experienced, and one that I had never even heard of being attempted before during a polygraph test. My next order of business was to have my English test questions translated and written down in both Thai and the mountain dialect. At this step, a seemingly insurmountable problem arose. I discovered that the first interpreter could neither read nor write.

The lack of written test questions was a problem. Test questions must be asked several times during polygraph testing to look for consistency in response from asking to asking. It is imperative that the questions be asked exactly the same each time to ensure that any reactions elicited are not due to different, unrehearsed words. The only way to ensure that questions are asked the same each time is to have them read to the examinee, exactly as previewed before testing.

In order to accomplish the agent's test, I had no choice but to have the questions read aloud in Thai to the first interpreter who then translated them in his mind to present the questions in the mountain dialect to the examinee. Since the questions were not written down by the first interpreter, I had no way of knowing whether they were verbalized the same from asking to asking. From a polygrapher's point of view, this was a horrible situation that threatened the validity of the examination. How could one analyze the charts? If I noted responses in the polygraph charts, how could I know whether they were due to deception to the question or due to being startled by the use of different words or phrases in the question? How could one evaluate and decide on the validity of a test like that when one of the basic principles of polygraph testing had to be violated in order to accomplish any testing? Although I was worried, I decided to proceed with the examination. There was no viable alternative, so I elected to see how it played out before I made any decision about the test's validity.

As the polygraph charts scrolled out during the examination, it was my responsibility to make notations to indicate when each questions began and ended, and when and what the examinee answered. I placed the question onset mark on the polygraph chart when the Thai interpreter started to read the question in Thai and then placed the question ending mark when the other interpreter finished the question in the mountain dialect. Based on the chart markings, each question appeared to be around fifteen seconds long. The normal length for a polygraph test question presented in English was around three or four seconds.

Although I reluctantly agreed to conduct the examination in this fashion, I must admit I originally thought it would be impossible to obtain conclusive results. Even though I thought it would be interesting to see how an examination conducted in this fashion would turn out, I was mentally prepared to issue an Inconclusive call before I even met the examinee.

The two-interpreter arrangement was certainly bizarre, but I could not have been more surprised by the clarity of the results. The charts obtained during the session were actually fairly good and seemed to clearly demonstrate he was being truthful about the location of the refinery and deceptive with regards to withholding knowledge about the location of other refineries. My polygraph report contained those conclusions, but I also cautioned that the results should be considered to be of low validity due to the unconventional use of two interpreters to conduct the case.

As peculiar as the two-interpreter case was, my experience with interpreters has been overwhelmingly favorable, and I have had very few bad experiences. When an interpreter is fluent, follows directions, and works with the polygraph examiner, conducting a case with an interpreter can be even more fun than a regular case, especially when interrogation is necessary. When using an interpreter during an interrogation, the examiner has time to mentally review the progress of the interrogation, develop a strategy for obtaining a confession, and formulate his next question while the interpreter is speaking. On the other hand, on three occasions my frustration with interpreters' lack of adequate language skill reached the point where I asked them to leave the room. Their Spanish was absolutely dreadful, and their constant mispronunciations and search for words prolonged the interviews and invalidated nearly every polygraph chart produced. Realizing that my limited Spanish was better than theirs, I finished the polygraph interviews by communicating directly with the agents in Spanish. All in all, my experience using interpreters has been very positive, but the case requiring the use of two interpreters was surely my strangest interpreter experience.

Chapter Twenty

Keep a Low Profile

Honesty pays, but it doesn't seem to pay
enough to suit some people.

—FRANK MCKINNEY HUBBARD

One of the basic tradecraft guidelines I followed during the conduct of covert operations polygraph cases overseas was to keep a low profile. It should be clearly evident that this is not a super-scientific, ultramodern type of tradecraft guideline. Keeping a low profile is a commonsense guideline. If you are going to engage in activity that could be interpreted as committing espionage in a foreign country and that could lead to your arrest and incarceration, not drawing attention to yourself as you engage in the activity is simply the application of good common sense. Any professional criminal would give you the very same advice. I tried to keep a low profile by blending in. For example, I did not wear a business suit to an examination that was scheduled to be conducted in a safe house located in the slums or down at the docks. I did not wear shorts and flip-flops to an examination to be conducted in a five-star hotel or a posh professional building. I tried to not stand out in a crowd, not draw attention to myself, and not create a scene.

Unfortunately, I have created scenes, had my best laid plans go wrong, and experienced the unexpected. It is most unfortunate when this occurs when I am on an espionage mission in a foreign country. I am an experienced world traveler with sound judgment, good decision-making skills, and good common sense. I always think that is a healthy self-assessment until I remind myself about my misadventure with a trainee, Tex, who accompanied me on a six-week-long TDY to South America. At the time, he was already an accomplished, competent examiner, but this trip was his introduction to covert operations polygraph work during an extended overseas trip. We were about halfway through the trip and on our last day of a five-day stay in one of my favorite South American locations. The city was a favorite for most visiting polygraph examiners. There were little shops and sidewalk cafés galore in the city, and most were located on a major street that was closed off to traffic. The street was the center of activity for the city's evening entertainment. There was a wide variety of excellent restaurants with extraordinarily scrumptious cuisine, and there were many movie theaters up and down the street. Also, there were street entertainers dazzling the crowds with music and dance on about every block of the mile-long street. The activities on this street made it an absolutely fantastic place to spend an evening during the trip. When we were not working at night, you could find us having a superb meal at an excellent restaurant and then either watching a new movie or strolling around the street.

As pleasant as all that was, there was an underlying tension in the atmosphere at all times. The city was well known for having its fair share of street demonstrations against the government. Every evening as we walked down the street on our way to restaurants and entertainment, we saw busloads of riot police parked in alleys waiting to spring into action if something happened. We also saw huge riot control vehicles that had gun turrets mounted on top that were actually water cannons. Nevertheless, as impressive looking as those vehicles, equipment, and riot police waiting for action were, every night everything was peaceful and calm. It did not take long to grow accustomed to their presence, and we soon totally ignored the show of force that just sat in the alleys.

On our last night in the city, we selected one of our favorite restaurants for our last dining experience. I think we were both looking forward to a quiet evening since we had to return to the hotel to get packed up for an early morning flight to our next stop. I'm sure the meal was excellent. All the meals during our stay were excellent. With full, satisfied stomachs, we stepped out of the restaurant into a cool evening, looking forward to a leisurely stroll back to our hotel. As we stood in the street, we could hear the distinct sound of a crowd's roar several blocks to our right.

Tex looked at me with a twinkle in his eye and said, "Let's go see what the ruckus is about."

"No, we should keep our distance," I replied, obviously displaying great control and wisdom beyond my years. It was a reply coming from an experienced world traveler with sound judgment, good decision-making skills, and good common sense. Then again, maybe I have an unrealistically high opinion of myself.

"Aw, come on. We'll just watch from afar," Tex pleaded.

"Well, okay," I said with reluctance.

We walked a couple of blocks toward the noise until we saw a huge mob of people milling about at a major intersection. We reached the edge of the crowd and started to mingle with hoards of people who were standing around, clogging the road, and chanting in Spanish. I could not understand what they were saying, but I was ready to hide my face and slink away if I heard something like, "Kill all Americans!" We could not see anything happening, so we pushed deeper into the crowd in order to get a better look up and down the street.

Suddenly and unexpectedly, the mob started moving. Since we were now in the heart of the mob, we had no choice but to move along with it. Everyone in the mob started running, and like it or not, we started running, too. There was no choice. We could either be trampled to death or we could run. We ran.

The roar of the mob behind us got louder. We could

hear a great deal of screaming and shouting. It was different than the chanting we heard before. As we ran down the street, I thought we should try to enter one of the stores, but I noticed all the stores were pulling down their iron grates and closing their doors. Ducking into a store to get out of harm's way was the only idea that came to mind as I ran down the street. So, fresh out of ideas, we had no choice but to keep on running with the crowd. As I ran, I could hear the engine noise from a large vehicle behind us, above the shouts of the crowd, and I assumed that the water cannon vehicles were being used for crowd control.

As we approached an intersection, we made our way to the right side of the mob and then abruptly turned right and stopped about ten feet from the running hoard of people, finally extracting ourselves from the mob. The mob kept going straight.

Tex said, "Let's just stand up against the wall. They're after the people who are running. They won't bother us. Just stand still. Let's stand up against the wall."

I was breathing hard from running, but I also felt energized by the excitement of the events. Tex and I had been laughing as we ran, but we both realized that we were in a dangerous predicament. I also knew that getting trampled to death by a riotous crowd, or shot and clubbed by riot control police, would make for an unpleasant evening.

Since I didn't have a better idea at the time, Tex's idea seemed to make sense. We plastered ourselves up against the brick wall of a building. I turned my face away from the crowd and stood very still. I could hear the mob move on down the street in the direction we had been running a minute before. Then I clearly heard the water cannon vehicle rumble to a stop in the intersection about fifty feet away. The engine in that vehicle was very loud, and it was close enough to us that the ground seemed to shake under our feet. Curiosity got the best of me. I quickly snapped my head around to get a look at what it was doing and saw a wall of water coming at me. I tried to turn quickly away but was instantly smashed up against the wall with a powerful stream of water. The stream knocked my head against the wall and soaked me from head to foot. I started to say something to Tex, but before I could utter a peep, a second wall of water hit us both. The riot control police must have been very proud of their target shooting success that day. We were completely drenched. As we stood there surveying the water damage to our bodies, we could hear the vehicle move on down the road after the running crowd.

At first, Tex and I just stood there, laughing at each other and at the predicament we had gotten ourselves into. The danger seemed to have passed, so we dripped, wrung out, and laughed. The laughing stopped when the itching started. Those diabolical riot control troops had some type of chemical mixed in with the water that made us itch wherever our clothes rubbed against our bodies. It started to get rather unpleasant so we decided to make our way back to the hotel to get showered and changed as quickly as we could.

There is never a good time to get water-cannoned, I guess, but unfortunately this episode happened on our last night in the country. Normally, when an examiner has an extended stay at a CIA office, travel documents and other valuables are stored at the office so they are not lost or stolen easily when the examiner travels around the city. Earlier that day when we left the office, we gathered together our important documents that we had stored in a safe. When the riot control police drenched us from head to foot that evening, our wallets, cash, traveler's checks, passports, and airline tickets were soaked.

We made our way back to the hotel that, unfortunately, was located about a mile up the street. It was an uncomfortable walk due to the annoying itching around our collars, cuffs, underwear, and socks. It drove us crazy. When we finally entered the hotel through the front lobby, the front desk staff could not help noticing two soaked, dripping Americans with miserable looks on their faces heading for the elevator. They instantly knew what had happened, and they thought it was incredibly hilarious. We suffered through a lot of finger pointing and loud guffawing as we walked past them to the elevator.

After I entered my hotel room, my clothes came off immediately. I showered in order to wash off the chemical that was causing me to itch. We had a taxi reserved in the morning to take us to the airport, so I had to dry out my clothes and belongings as quickly as I could in order to get packed for the next day's travel. I had to hang my soaked clothes in the bathroom, hoping they would dry a bit before packing them in the morning. I had money, traveler's checks, and airline tickets spread all over the hotel room in an attempt to air-dry them. They were draped on lamp-shades, chairbacks, and windowsills. It sounds comical now, but I was a bit miserable at the time.

I heard Tex tell his version of this story at the Federal Interagency Polygraph Seminar one year. In his version, he alleged I was the one who said, "Let's go see what all the ruckus is about." Tex has never been one to let the truth interfere with the telling of a good story.

I always tried to keep a low profile on every one of my overseas trips to avoid the unwanted attention of foreign government officials. I did not always succeed. However, I'm not the only polygrapher who has encountered problems while trying to operate in a clandestine manner. I have a friend who once told me his tale of a nightmarish, albeit comical situation he encountered while conducting a case in a safe house located in an apartment building in South America. He said he might as well have arrived at the building leading a big brass band to announce his arrival and then shot off cannons from the balcony to broadcast his exact location.

The safe house was located in a rather modern apartment complex. The complex was composed of four apartment buildings arranged in a circle, so a courtyard area was formed in the center of the four buildings. The courtyard contained a park and a playground for children, so it was the ideal gathering place for many residents. After entering the apartment, the examiner discovered it to be well outfitted and an almost ideal location for a polygraph interview. When he surveyed the apartment, he determined the best place to conduct the examination was in the dining room. He set up the polygraph equipment on the dining room table and rearranged furniture so that everyone would have proper seats. The outside wall of the dining room did not have traditional windows. The entire length of the twelve-foot wall had louvered glass panes that were slanted open. He looked out through the louvers and saw that the courtyard below was filled with people. He then looked straight out at the apartment building directly across from the one he was situated in. He noticed he could see into some of the living rooms and dining rooms that did not have curtains drawn and realized that everyone in the apartment building across the way had a clear look into the dining room he planned to use for the polygraph session.

Seeking a remedy for that glaring security issue, he first noticed there were no curtains in the dining room to cover the louvered glass panes but then saw Venetian blinds near the ceiling. Thinking it would be a simple matter to lower the blinds to block the view, he stepped up on one of the dining room chairs and started to pull on the Venetian blind cords. They seemed to be stuck, as they did not budge an inch, so he pulled harder. As he yanked with more force, the twelve-foot section of Venetian blinds suddenly came crashing down, slipped right through the window louvers to the outside, and smacked the side of the building with a deafening metallic noise as the examiner desperately hung on to the cord. The Venetian blinds, with a length almost twice the height of the examiner, weighed more than the examiner. He was almost pulled through the window louvers with the blinds. As he hung half out of the window, he looked down and saw that every face in the courtyard was staring up at him as the Venetian blinds smacked again and again against the side of the building.

Keeping a low profile sounds like it should be a simple task to accomplish, but it actually can be awfully difficult to do. Another friend of mine once told me the story of a rather bizarre situation he encountered in a South American city. His story involved conducting a test in a case officer's residence, an apartment located in a multistoried building.

When the test was over, the examiner packed up the polygraph equipment and left with the case officer. They took the elevator down to the lobby and walked to the parking lot where the case officer's car was parked. After he stowed his gear and got into the car, the examiner realized he left a paperback novel he had been reading in the officer's apartment. He told the case officer he was going to make a quick trip back to the apartment to retrieve the book. He walked back to the building and rode the elevator up to the appropriate floor. He walked down the hallway, stopped at the apartment, and knocked on the front door. There was no answer. He knew the case officer's wife had been in the apartment when he left. Thinking she was too busy with something inside to hear his knock, he tried the doorknob and was surprised to discover the door to be unlocked. He slowly pushed the door open and called inside. No one answered. It was now dark in the apartment. All the lights had been on when he left only a few minutes earlier. Although confused by the dark apartment that now confronted him, he knew exactly what he wanted and where it was located. He slowly walked toward the living room in the darkened apartment but stopped dead in his tracks when he saw a naked man in an easy chair with a naked woman kneeling in front of him. The naked man visibly tensed when he noticed the examiner approaching. His hands left his grasp on the naked woman, and his eyes bugged out like a startled owl. The naked woman, with her back toward the examiner, didn't notice him at all. She was quite occupied and fully engaged in her task. The naked man glared angrily at the examiner and started to rise out of the chair. Stunned at the unexpected sight of such intimate activity, the examiner was temporarily immobilized. He realized he had somehow burst into the wrong apartment. Not able to speak Spanish, he blurted out, "Wrongo hacienda. *Adiós!*" He spun around and ran out of the apartment as rapidly as his legs would take him. He sprinted down the hallway, rode the elevator down to the lobby, and ran to the case officer's car. Upon entering the car, he advised the case officer to make a speedy departure to avoid the police that were undoubtedly on their way.

My friends managed to bring a lot of unwanted attention upon themselves. The last thing you want when trying to keep a low profile is uninvited interest in your activities. Unfortunately, this seems to occur too often. I once discovered that something as simple as a passport can create a scene. But then again, my passport was unusual. Blank pages in a passport are used for visas and entry and exit stamps. A visa is stamped in the passport by host government officials to give the traveler permission to enter a country for a designated period of time. A visa usually takes up half a page, sometimes a full page, and contains signatures, dates, and numbers. When a traveler goes through immigration at airports, an entry stamp is placed in the passport on arrival and an exit stamp is recorded on departure. Those stamps are much smaller than the visa stamp. Many of them will fit on the page of a passport. The typical American traveler does not undertake a sufficient number of trips during the life of a passport to accumulate enough visas and entry/exit stamps to fill up all the pages in a passport. When a traveler manages to complete a great deal of foreign travel prior to the expiration of a passport, pages of the passport can fill up with all of the visa stamps and entry/exit stamps. When this happens, the traveler is issued a page extender, an accordion-like group of pages that is sealed to one of the existing passport pages. Each accordion pull-out adds an additional twelve blank passport pages.

From 1976 through 1979, I was a regional polygraph examiner stationed in the Far East. I traveled quite a bit of the time to other Far East and Southeast Asian countries. Actually, I once figured out that I was away from home 40 percent of the time during the three-year tour. On one of my trips from my home base, an immigration official at the international airport looked through my passport in search of a visa for my destination country. He simply wanted to make sure my passport was in order so that I wouldn't be sent on a flight back home if I failed to have a visa giving me permission to visit the country. He flipped through the pages looking at visa after visa, but was unsuccessful in finding the applicable visa. His search through the pages brought him to an accordion. He searched all the pages of the accordion and still couldn't find the visa. He looked up at me quizzically and then continued with his search through the pages of the passport. He came across a second accordion. He searched all twelve pages of the second accordion but still couldn't find the visa. He looked long and hard at me again. I could have indicated where the visa was located, but I felt he wouldn't think kindly if I snatched the passport out of his hands. He continued searching the passport pages without success and then came across a third accordion. He unfolded the pages, searched all twelve of them, but still couldn't find the visa. He looked up at me again with a sour look on his face. He continued searching until he came across a fourth accordion. He searched all twelve of its pages and still failed to find the visa. He finally looked through the last several pages in the passport without success. The whole process had taken considerable time. I felt awfully uncomfortable and noticed that the people standing behind me in line were very impatient and very curious about the holdup. Several onlookers crowded around the official's counter to watch the proceedings. I grew increasingly unnerved by the ruckus the affair was causing. Through no fault of my own, I wasn't keeping a low profile.

In an obvious expression of disgust, the official tossed

my passport down on the counter, looked me straight in the eye, pointed an accusing finger at me, and said quite loudly, "You work for the CIA!" There must have been twelve sets of eyes and ears nearby who witnessed the official's accusatory words.

In the interrogation business, this approach is known as a Direct Positive Confrontation. The official had attempted to catch me off guard with the bluntness of his accusation and overwhelm me with his belief in my guilt. His words were designed to elicit a response from me that he could analyze. He wanted to see how I would react both physically and verbally. Unfortunately, I wasn't expecting such an approach from an airport immigration official. He caught me totally off guard and completely unprepared to issue an appropriate response.

This would be an excellent place in my tale to insert a lie in order to present myself in a more favorable light. I could say I responded with a cool, suave, debonair, James Bond–like answer—something like, "My good man, please stop joking and finish with my passport." That would have been a calm, collected way to respond when an accusing finger was thrust in my face, and I desperately needed to be perceived as being innocent. Actually, I did manage to recover a little bit after my initial stammering and say, "CIA? No. Only in the movies. Let me show you where that visa is in my passport." Although the official let me proceed after inspecting the visa, the fact that my passport threatened my ability to keep a low profile was alarming.

My passport was issued to me by my own government to identify and protect me, not to put me in harm's way.

Though I felt like running, I walked from the immigration officer's booth toward the departure lounge. I needed to fold up the passport's four accordions that the officer left in disarray. When I found a seat, I looked at my passport with its dozens of pages containing visas for all the countries in which I have applied my espionage craft. Hundreds of entry and exit stamps represented trips to test and interrogate foreign spies. Reflecting on my many travels, I thought of exotic cities, friendly people, and delicious food. However, these were not vacations. I had a job to do. With my work came high-speed car chases, surveillance by hostile intelligence services, blown clandestine agent meetings, double agents, interrogations by immigration officials, surreptitious hotel room searches, teargassing by riot police, and confrontations with soldiers armed with submachine guns.

The immigration officer wasn't the first one to nearly nab me. He never knew how close he came to catching a real "spy."

Epilogue

Lord, Lord, how this world is given to lying!
—WILLIAM SHAKESPEARE

In the great lobby of CIA Headquarters in Langley, Virginia, there is a memorial to honor CIA's best that have fallen in service to their country. The memorial is dramatic in its simplicity. Gray stars engraved on a white marble wall are bordered by the U.S. flag and the CIA flag. On a table below the stars lies an open book listing names of the honored and the year of their passing. Sometimes, there is a blank space where the name should be as, for some, their anonymity survives them even in death. Having one of these stars is the greatest honor the CIA can bestow on one of its own.

Over many years, I watched the number of stars on the

wall grow. Currently, 111 stars represent CIA's unsung heroes that gave their all protecting our country. I am honored to have known 3 of them. The CIA's Memorial Wall is a somber reminder that a career in intelligence is dangerous.

My story is just one man's story. Thousands have chosen careers with the CIA over the decades. People of the highest caliber—dedicated, well-educated, sacrificing, patriotic souls—join the Agency each year. Each one of these shadow warriors knows the work is dangerous. Employment with the CIA is not a job; it is a lifestyle often filled with trials and tribulations. Many employees live undercover, forbidden to identify their true employer or reveal their real profession. Their families must also live undercover, requiring daily lies and deception to maintain it. Many CIA employees, especially those involved in overseas covert operations, live a lifestyle fraught with deception and danger.

My forty years with the CIA certainly had its ups and downs but, without equivocation, I can say it was fun. It was a grand and glorious adventure with a lifestyle I willingly embraced. There is an old saying that goes, "Work is only work if you'd rather be doing something else." To me, doing something else for a living was inconceivable.

Thirty years ago, I advised a group of senior polygraph examiners to record their adventures from around the world as covert ops polygraph examiners. Many of them are gone now. Their stories are lost forever. I can remember few details, but I certainly remember listening with admiration, amazement, fear, and amusement. Now, as the retired paladin of polygraph, I finally took my own advice and that of countless students, fellow examiners, and instructors and wrote down my own adventures. It is my hope that my story entertains but also helps keep others in the world of espionage and covert activities safe from harm.

The CIA became a part of my life when my father signed on with the Agency in 1952. I was only four years old. My family began the typical CIA nomadic life. Following my father's assignments to fascinating destinations created a wanderlust that calls to me even now. In 1971, I signed on with the Agency and soon began what eventually became a thirty-eight-year career in polygraph. For sure, the most exciting and rewarding years were those involved with covert ops polygraph. For sixty years, the CIA has been part of my life. Sixty years! Mine has truly been a life of lies and spies.